BONES

R. McNeill Alexander
Professor of Zoology
The University of Leeds

PHOTOGRAPHY BY
Brian Kosoff

FOREWORD BY
Mark A. Norell
American Museum of
Natural History

ILLUSTRATIONS BY
Edward Heck

BONES

The Unity of Form and Function

Westview Press
A Member of the Perseus Books Group

A PETER N. NEVRAUMONT BOOK

Find us on the World Wide Web at www.westviewpress.com

Published by Westview Press
A Member of the Perseus Books Group
First Edition Published by Macmillan, 1994

A CIP catalog record for this book is available from the Library of
Congress.
ISBN 0-8133-3806-9

Printed in China

Created and produced by
Nevraumont Publishing Company
New York, New York

Ann J. Perrini, *President*

Scientific Adviser: Mark A. Norell,
American Museum of Natural History
Technical Adviser: Henry Galiano,
Maxilla & Mandible Ltd., New York
Book Design: José Conde, Kanazawa City, Japan

FIGURE A (half title)

Human skeleton
Homo sapiens
Differences between human skeletons
and those of other mammals reflect
our peculiarities—large brains,
dexterous hands and bipedal stance.

PLATE 1 (frontispiece)

The jaws of a Gorilla.
Gorilla gorilla

Contents

Foreword by Mark A. Norell 6

CHAPTER 1 · *Introduction* 10

CHAPTER 2 · *Strength with Lightness* 24

CHAPTER 3 · *Joints* 58

CHAPTER 4 · *Muscle Attachments* 80

CHAPTER 5 · *Mechanisms* 100

CHAPTER 6 · *Teeth* 114

CHAPTER 7 · *Acoustic Bones* 144

CHAPTER 8 · *Designs That Grow* 166

CHAPTER 9 · *Patterns and Textures* 192

CHAPTER 10 · *Epilogue: Function and Beauty* 210

Photographer's Statement 219

Index 220

Acknowledgments 223

Foreword

MY father is an engineer. Like all builders, he has both a fondness and an appreciation for how things are constructed. My own field of vertebrate paleontology, the study of fossil bones, is very different. Yet, each livelihood revolves around structural elements. My father's concentrates on metal, wood, concrete and architectural adaptations to the forces of stress and strain. Biologists like R. McNeill Alexander and me, concern ourselves with the bones of vertebrate bodies and the evolutionary response of animals with backbones to physical and historical forces.

The similarities between fields as disparate as engineering and biology go farther. The evolution of architecture emulates the historical construction of organisms that results in the myriad diversity of animal types. That is what this book is about. As you will read, basic engineering principles (force, stress, strain and tension), their mechanical solutions (hinges, joints, arches and trusses) and the characteristics of materials (hardness, flexibility, and the combinational qualities of composites and laminates) are just as relevant to the body of an organism as to the design of a racing sailboat. The correspondence is so great that one could easily imagine that the principles of structural architecture were discovered by careful observation of organisms by ancient engineers. I cite (among other things) the correspondence between the ribs of vertebrate bodies and the framing of canoes, ships, tents and houses. All are the same engineering response to the common problem of providing support and lightness; but we know that evolution solved the problem hundreds of millions of years before we did.

No matter what precipitated the great ideas in architecture, both bodies and buildings are subject to equivalent physical forces requiring identical solutions. Consequently, heavy bodies are supported by heavy legs, and large buildings with large columns. Such examples are manifest and underscore the elegant explanatory power of simple engineering principles applied in this book to the design of animals.

It is not the constructive principles explaining vertebrate form and function that occupy my workday. Instead it is the interrelationship of life's diverse elements. The nexus between what McNeill Alexander presents here and what I do is based on history. The morphology of animals is a result of two powerful forces—construction and legacy. The study of this legacy is called systematics. This is the business of making detailed family trees of organisms based on evidence of the shared presence of evolutionary novelties. I try to do this in a repeatable and empirical fashion, so my ideas can be continually tested by the addition of more information.

The relationship between construction and genealogy can be summed up in a line from an old reggae tune: "in this great future you can't forget your past." This means that the way things are is directly related to what they came from. In biological terms this severely limits the sorts of architectural gimmicks organisms can employ. If we look at evolution as a constant process of alteration, modification and rearrangement, the end products that we call organisms are contingent on what was initially there to be altered, rearranged or modified. It is unlikely that an organism like a jellyfish would ever directly evolve wings and be able to fly. Why? Powered flight requires rigid wings to generate lift. Jellyfish lack solid supporting skeletons, causing them to be reduced to a glob of protoplasm when they are removed from their supportive aquatic environment; hence their name. Instead, powered flight is restricted to animals whose direct ancestors have hard parts. These hard parts, like the exoskeleton of insects and the arm bones of vertebrates, were co-opted during the course of evolution to form wings. The sequence of hard parts, wings and powered flight is a relatively simple example. Nevertheless, the relationships among history, structure, diversity and the mechanics of organisms are important ones that are illuminated only through understanding genealogy.

Without vertebrate hard parts—bones, the title of this book—our appreciation for the diversity of life would be substantially diminished. Bones are hard parts. Hard parts form fossils. Fossils are our window to the history of our relatives on this planet. Without these fossils we would have no record of giant dinosaurs, mammoths or even our own near ancestors like Lucy. Fossil bones tell us two obvious things. First, they broaden the spectrum of physical types that have been present during life's history available to us for study. More importantly, for my own interests, they capture a hard physical record of transformational stages between organisms.

We biologists are left knowing that we see today only a fraction of the number of animals that have occupied our planet. Some paleontologists have estimated that the known fossils represent only 1 percent of the total number of species ever to have lived. This is vastly optimistic. Biologists have named over a million species of extant organisms. Current estimates suggest that the actual number is more than an order of magnitude greater. That's over ten million species in a single geologic instant. If we assume that diversities in the past were roughly similar to those in the present, we see just how deficient the fossil record is. Only about 100,000 species of fossil organisms have been named for all of life's 3.7 billion year history. This has important connotations on the ideas presented in this book because it greatly increases the amount of structural diversity that must be considered. A striking example is the relationship of mechanical modifications of skeleton and muscle to size. If our upper limit on size of a terrestrial animal were calibrated on today's largest, the African elephant, our conception of size would be much different from what it is when the upper limit is set to include the giant extinct sauropod dinosaurs like *Ultrasaurus* and *Seismosaurus.* Although they are impossible to measure accurately with only fragmentary fossils available, these lumbering giants weighed on the order of almost ten times that of the largest elephant.

Aside from demonstrating that living animals are only a fractional subset of life, fossils also provide direct clues about the links between species. There are a couple of issues involved here. What the fossil record captures is a history of the characteristics that are present in animals today. That is not to say that these fossil animals are direct ancestors of living animals. Direct ancestry is a nefarious concept among biologists of my generation. Modern systematics portrays animals as related by kinship, concentrating on closest relatives rather than ancestors. Consequently, we do not claim that *Archaeopteryx,* the archetypal protobird, is a direct ancestor of pigeons. But *Archaeopteryx* still tells us much about pigeon evolution. Because it preserves a mosaic of characteristics—some primitive like a long tail and teeth, and some bird-like feathers and wings—it tells us much about the transition between extinct dinosaurs and living dinosaurs (i.e., birds).

A more ethereal issue concerns the use of structures. This is one place where biology departs from architectural engineering. Unlike buildings which are fabricated from ground up according to a blueprint, organisms need to function while they are under construction. Evolution, therefore, is not a purposeful or directed pathway toward some particular end. At each stage of the game features need to function. That is not to say that evolution operates in such a way that every attribute of an organism has a definite or continuous function. Instead, features during any particular stage of evolution (or development and growth) cannot be dysfunctional. It is in this area where the blanket covered by McNeill Alexander's and my interests becomes even more expansive, encompassing the disciplines of development, genetics and even philosophy.

My study of these issues, however, represents something much more basic than pure academic interest. I have always appreciated the aesthetic aspects of vertebrate bones. Consequently, I have always been drawn to natural history museums. Much of my daily existence as a curator of vertebrate paleontology is filled with bones. My passion is not weird, especially when one considers that the American Museum of Natural History draws over two million visitors a year, and that the most popular exhibits are based on bones. Directly across New York's Central Park from our institution is the Metropolitan Museum of Art. There, where traditionally aesthetics have been held at a higher premium, bones are everywhere—from the paintings of Georgia O'Keefe to the sculpture of Rodin. It really was as basic as my enjoyment of the way bones look that drew me to work on this book.

I feel that what McNeill Alexander has produced in *Bones* is a sort of *The Way Things Work* goes to the menagerie. At the risk of saying something about my attention span, I will admit that I rarely buy books without illustration. We are visual animals. No matter how good a book about objects is, these objects cannot be adequately described without pictures. Alexander's use of Brian Kosoff's precise photographs combined with an ingenious text make this work both an admirable piece of scholarship and a beautiful object celebrating the rich history and diversity of vertebrate design.

Mark A. Norell
Associate Curator
Department of Vertebrate Paleontology
American Museum of Natural History

Chapter 1

INTRODUCTION

——————

I GREW up in the smell of burning bones. One mile west of my childhood home was a factory where bones were reduced to ash for use as a phosphate fertilizer. The smoke poured out of the factory chimney, and when the wind blew from the west the smell was disgusting.

Bones are associated much more with death than with bad smells (though the two can go together). The skeleton of a cow, bleached by the sun in the semi-desert of northern Kenya, is a powerful symbol of thirst and famine. The charnel houses of Brittany, France, full of bones dug up a few centuries ago to make more room in overcrowded churchyards, are macabre reminders of human mortality. The bones carved on some old tombstones are quainter and more comfortable symbols of death, and the pirate skull and crossbones has lost its terror, making us think of exciting stories and childish games.

Foul smells and death represent the bad image of bones. In this book, we will look at bones much more positively, as strange and beautiful objects and above all as marvels of engineering design. Look at the snake skeleton [PLATE 2] with its slender, elegantly curved ribs each almost exactly like the one in front but with the shapes changing progressively along the length of the body. Isn't that beautiful? Look at the chameleon skull [PLATE 3] with the horns on its snout. Isn't that bizarre? For the moment we look merely at their strangeness and beauty, but this book is concerned mainly with the functions of bones in living animals, and with their design.

PLATE 2

Skeleton of a Reticulated Python.
Python reticulatus
Each vertebra and rib is almost, but not exactly, like the next.

PLATE 4

(left) Pin and ring game.
Amerindian (Ojibway)
The beads have been cut from bird
leg bones. The game was to catch the
perforated plate on the pin.

(right) Necklace of salmon vertebrae
with a pendant wooden ring.
Amerindian (Shoshone, nineteenth
century)
Both in the game and in the necklace,
bones are used as decorative beads.

PLATE 3

Skull of a horned chameleon.
Chameleo oweni
The three horns point forward from
the snout and the eye socket is on the
side of the skull, below the museum
catalogue number.

The word "design" may suggest a Creator figuring out the best way to build a snake. I do not know whether there is a Creator (the scientific methods that I am accustomed to using are incapable of deciding the question) and I have a very different concept of the design of skeletons. This is design by evolution, a powerful and apparently inevitable process that molds the structures of animals to suit their ways of life. In his book *Fossils: The Evolution and Extinction of Species* Niles Eldredge has explained the theory of evolution and presented some of the evidence of the process, provided by bones fossilized at various times over the past 500 million years.

In writing about design by evolution, I will sometimes use language that some biologists would criticize. For example, I may say that stags have antlers for fighting with. My critics would say I should not write like that unless I want to imply a Creator with a sense of purpose, designing antlers for fighting. My answer is that if antlers evolved because stags with antlers were more successful in fights with rival males, and so left more offspring than stags without antlers, surely they are for fighting.

We will use the rest of this chapter to think about design. Later in the book we will be concerned with the design of bones in relation to the uses that the animals make of them, but here I introduce some of the principles of design by looking at uses that people have made of animal bones.

Bones are plentiful in most cultures, as waste from food. For American Indians they made (among other things) decorative beads. For this purpose, many different bones would do; choosing between salmon vertebrae and bird leg bones [both in PLATE 4] may be a matter merely of availability and taste.

For some purposes, the shapes of particular bones may make them much more suitable than other bones. This is reflected in the names of the bones of the lower leg, the tibia and fibula. Tibia was the Latin name for the shinbone, but it also meant flute, and the Latin word fibula meant pin. European archaeologists have found many Roman and later flutes made from tibias of sheep and of birds such as cranes or geese. They have also found plenty of pins from the Early Christian and Viking periods, carved from fibulas of pigs.

Any long, straight, hollow bone will make a flute. American Indians made flutes from bird wing bones as well as leg bones. A human femur (thighbone) would not be my choice of material, but the flute made from it [PLATE 5] presumably works well. To make a pin for fastening clothing, a long slender bone with a knob at one end is needed, and pigs' fibulas are like that. Sheep rather than pig tibias were used for flutes, presumably because they are longer, but the fibulas of sheep have been reduced in the course of evolution to small nodules of bone that would be no use for pin making.

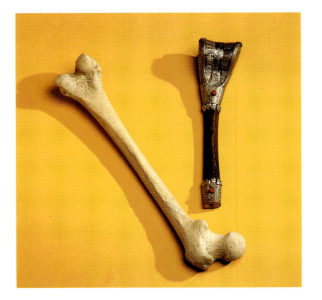

PLATE 5

Two human femurs (thigh bones), one
of them used to make a flute with
silver mounts.
Homo sapiens
The flute was purchased in Thailand.
Any long, hollow bone will serve to
make a flute.

Sometimes, a chance resemblance to something else may suggest a use
for a bone. There are seven vertebrae in the neck of a horse, each differently
shaped from the next, and one of them (the sixth) happens to be shaped like
the head and trunk of a man with upraised arms. Examples are occasionally
found as ornaments in English cottages, painted with a face and a preacher's
gown. They are known as Wesleys after the great eighteenth-century evange-
list John Wesley, who founded the Methodist Church.

Another example of a bone being chosen for its shape comes from science
rather than country crafts. Some chameleons have horns on their snouts
[PLATE 3] though most (like other kinds of reptiles) do not. Lindsey
Harkness was a graduate student who wanted to find out how reptiles use
their eyes to judge the distances of objects. She chose to study chameleons
that feed on insects, catching them by flicking out their long, sticky tongues: a
chameleon only 17 centimeters (7 inches) long from snout to vent can extend
its tongue to an extraordinary 25 centimeters (10 inches). The tongue shoots
out so fast, in about one twenty-fifth of a second, that there is no time for the
animal to make any correction if its initial aim turns out to have been inaccu-
rate. Therefore, it needs to be able to judge distance as well as direction.
There were two hypotheses about how this might be done. One hypothesis
was that chameleons judge distance by comparing the images in their left and
right eyes: the closer an object is, the greater the difference in the angles from
which the two eyes see it. The other was that the clue to distance is the degree

PLATE 6

Jaws of a Rough-toothed Dolphin,
with scrimshaw decoration.
Steno bredanensis
Nineteenth century. The flags
are British.

PLATE 7

(*top*) Hide flesher made from Moose cannon bone.
Amerindian (Ute, nineteenth century)
(*bottom*) Skinning knife made from Caribou tibia.
Amerindian (Tahltan, nineteenth century)
Where hides are prepared, bone is available, and is an obvious choice of material for making tools.

to which the eyes have to be focused. Harkness chose to test these rival hypotheses by altering the chameleon's vision in ways that would affect its judgment of distance differently, depending on which theory was correct. She did this by fitting the lizards with spectacles, and made the delightful decision to use a species with horns on its snout because that made it easier to attach them. Horned chameleons wearing spectacles with converging lenses (as used by far-sighted people) overestimated the distances of flies and ones with diverging lenses (as used for short sight) underestimated distance. These results supported the hypothesis that chameleons use the degree to which the eye has to be focused as the principal clue for judging distance.

The horse vertebra happened to be a suitable shape to represent a preacher and the chameleon horn was conveniently shaped to carry spectacles, but design is not merely a matter of convenient shape: availability and material properties are often predominantly important. The bones used as beads [PLATE 4] were not only plentiful: they were also durable, yet much easier to cut or bore to make beads than stone (for example) would have been.

The dolphin's jaws decorated by a whaler [PLATE 6] were also available, durable and easily worked. They are fine ornaments, and (probably more important) they kept their maker occupied in the long intervals in a voyage in which no whales may have been sighted.

Bone is an excellent material for making tools to prepare hides: if you have fresh hides, you also have bones. The skinning knife [PLATE 7, *bottom*] could

not be made sharp enough to cut through skin, but if that were done first with a stone blade this bone tool would be strong and stiff enough for the rest of the job. To make one, a large straight bone is needed, preferably one with a flat surface: the tibia of a caribou was an obvious choice. The other tool, a hide flesher [PLATE 7, *top*], was used for scraping the inner surface of the hide. The knuckle end was used as a handle, and there is a serrated scraping edge at the other end. Not much work was needed to form this tool from a cannon bone, and (if metal were too expensive or not available) it is hard to think of a better material than bone. Pottery would have been too brittle, wood would have lost its edge when damp and a stone scraper would have been harder to make.

Antler has properties that make it better than ordinary bone for some jobs. We will learn in Chapter 2 that it is no stronger than ordinary bone but is a little more flexible, which makes it better able to withstand the knocks when rival stags fight for hinds. This same flexibility makes it less likely to break if it is used for making tools that have to withstand impacts.

Antler picks were used by some of the earliest British miners. Grime's Graves are a group of Neolithic (about 4,000 years ago) flint mines in Norfolk. There are remains of several hundred shafts, dug down through chalk to a layer of flint at depths of up to 40 feet (12 meters). From the bottom of each shaft, tunnels radiate out into the flint that was mined for making axes and other sharp implements. Many picks made from antlers have been found in the mines: they were presumably used for loosening the chalk and levering out lumps of flint. The antlers came from red deer, a close relative of American elk. They made better picks than the caribou antler [PLATE 8] would have done: their tines (branches) were simple spikes, and each pick was made simply by cutting off all the tines but one.

A spear thrower is not designed for hitting things with, but an antler spear thrower [PLATE 9] should be better than one made from bone at withstanding the rough and tumble of hunting. It was presumably used in the way that Australian aboriginals use similar gadgets, to increase the effective length of a thrower's arm, enabling the spear to be thrown faster and farther. The Australians fit the blunt end of the spear into the cupped end of the thrower, and hold the other end of the thrower. The carved horse may have had some magical significance: wild horses were speared and eaten, not ridden.

Succeeding chapters discuss the design of bones and skeletons, considering not only shapes and materials but also costs in relation to the functions that the bones serve in living animals. Our subject will be biology but many of the ideas and experimental methods we will discuss are taken from engineering

PLATE 8

Caribou (Reindeer) antler.
Rangifer tarandus (late Palaeolithic, about 12,000 years ago)
Antler is a good material for making tools that have to withstand impacts.

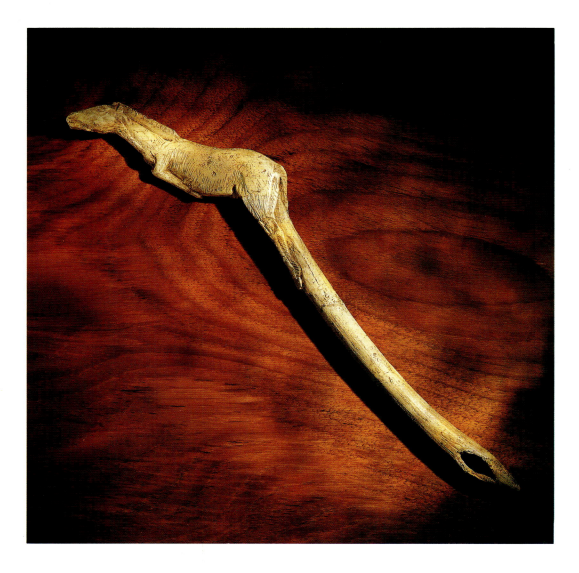

PLATE 9

Spear thrower made from Red Deer
antler.
Cervus elaphus
Magdalenian period (late Palaeolithic,
about 18,000 years ago)

PLATE 10

Model dinosaur skeleton.
Tyrannosaurus rex (Cretaceous period,
about 70 million years ago)
Real skeletons are about 8.5 meters
(28 feet) long, and the living adult
animal is estimated to have weighed
7 tons.

mechanics. We have already mentioned engineering concepts such as strength and stiffness without stopping to consider precisely what they mean. Their meanings, and the meanings of other technical terms, will have to be made clear in later chapters.

It may seem strange that a book about bones should depend so much on engineering, but there is a good reason. If you wanted to assess the design of a bridge you would consult an engineer. She or he would calculate the stresses in its girders and suspension cables, and consider whether their shapes and thicknesses were appropriate to the jobs they had to do. The choice of material would also have to be considered, taking account of strength, durability, availability and cost. Similar analysis can help us to understand the design of a *Tyrannosaurus* skeleton [PLATE 10]. If you wanted to understand the workings of an old-style railway signal box you would again consult an engineer, who would be able to explain how the levers, cables and pulleys interacted to raise and lower the signals and operate the switches. Similar explanations are needed to explain the mechanism whereby rattlesnakes erect their fangs to strike and some fishes extend their jaws as long sucking tubes. Engineering is the science of structure, material and movement, developed mainly for designing man-made structures and mechanisms, but it can also help us to understand the structures and mechanisms of animals. An anatomist who ignores engineering mechanics is missing one of the most powerful resources of human knowledge.

PLATE 11

Whalebone from the mouth of a
Blue Whale.
Balaenoptera musculus
This is horn, not bone. The fringes
served as strainers, to capture the
small crustaceans that the whale ate.

Bone is found only in vertebrate animals: fishes, amphibians, reptiles, birds and mammals. Some other animals such as insects, crustaceans and mollusks also have skeletons, but they are made of different materials, distinct from bone. Even among vertebrates (animals with backbones), there are other skeletal materials as well as bone, such as the cartilage which forms the skeletons of sharks and the horn which covers the hooves and horns of antelopes. Whalebone [PLATE 11], despite its name, is not bone, but fish scales [PLATE 128], surprisingly, are bone. When we learn about the composition of bone in the next chapter we will be able to see how cartilage, horn and whalebone differ from it. Teeth and tusks consist mainly of dentine (ivory), a material that is closely similar to bone, so this book about bones has a chapter about them.

The plan of the book is this. In the next chapter, we will discuss the strengths of bones. First we will examine the composition of bone (the material) to discover why it is strong. Then we will consider how thick bones ought to be, to be strong enough without being cumbersome, and how they should be constructed to combine strength with lightness in the best possible way. Chapters 3 and 4 are about the joints between bones, and about how bones are moved by muscles. After that we will be ready to discuss, in Chapter 5, some mechanisms formed by bones jointed together—for example, the elaborate mechanisms of fish jaws [PLATE 71]. Teeth are the subject of Chapter 6, where we will examine examples ranging from the cutting blades of piranhas to the grinding molars of cattle. We will then make an abrupt change of topic, to look in Chapter 7 at bones concerned with sound production and hearing, including the breast bones of cranes and the tiny bones inside our ears. The science of acoustics will help us to understand how they function. Next, in Chapter 8, we will think about a problem that does not arise in conventional engineering but is crucial in biology: bones must be able to grow as the body grows, and must remain strong and functional throughout the animal's life. Chapter 9 is about patterns in skeletons, both patterns formed by groups of bones (such as the repeating pattern of the ribs in the snake skeleton) [PLATE 2], and patterns on bones (such as the texture of the rough surfaces on the chameleon skull) [PLATE 3]. Finally, an Epilogue looks back at the book as a whole, showing how principles that have been explained in separate chapters may all apply to a single skull.

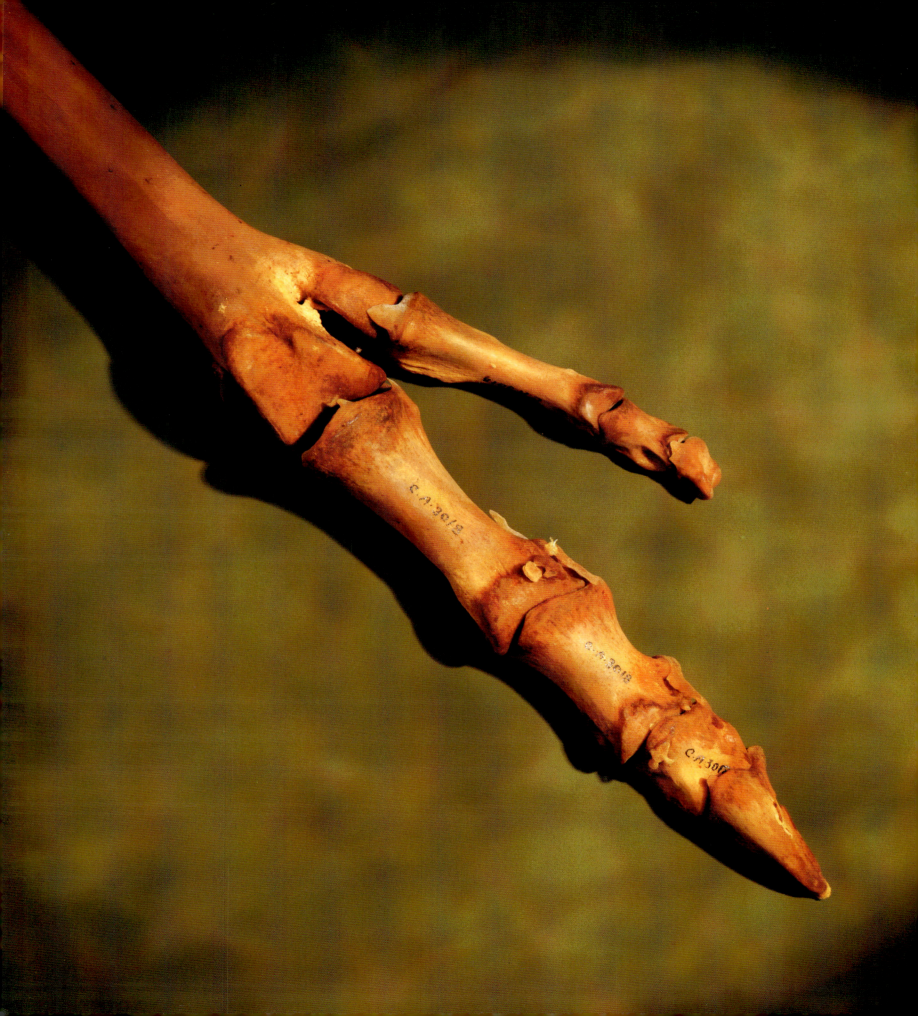

Chapter 2

STRENGTH WITH LIGHTNESS

———

LOOK at the long, slender bones in the foot of an ostrich [PLATE 12]. They are strong but light and have to be both to enable this large bird to run fast. In this chapter we will ask how strength combined with lightness is achieved. We will compare bone, the material, with strong, light engineering materials such as fiberglass. We will ask how bone can be used to best advantage in building bones, and we will find out why so many bones are hollow. We will examine some very fragile bones in the nose of a sea otter and some massively strong bones in the legs of an extinct bird. A bone can always be strengthened by making it heavier or lightened by making it weaker, so we will think about the best possible compromise between strength and lightness.

For the present, however, we return to the fast-running ostrich with its strong, light leg bones. I have driven over open grassland in Kenya, filming a running ostrich as it ran alongside us. We had to drive alarmingly fast and were badly jolted when we went over a hollow and all four wheels left the ground. Just before that, our speedometer was reading 16 meters per second (36 miles per hour). That is much faster than the best human sprinters, who reach 11 meters per second (25 miles per hour) at the mid-point of a 100 meter (110 yard) sprint, and a little faster than any of my records of antelope speeds. It is even fast enough to give the bird a chance in a horse race: times given in newspapers tell us that most horse races are won at speeds between

PLATE 12

Foot skeleton of an Ostrich.
Struthio camelus
The Ostrich is the fastest running bird, and has lightly-built feet.

16 and 17 meters per second (36-38 miles per hour). In such fast running, strides are long and each foot can be on the ground for only a small fraction of the stride time. This implies large forces for the following reason. When I stand still with my weight equally shared by my legs, the force on each foot is half my body weight. When I run, each foot still supports half my weight but does this by exerting a much larger force for the small fraction of the time that it is on the ground. Records from force-sensitive plates set into the ground show that the feet of human sprinters exert peak forces of about 3.5 times bodyweight, and I calculate from the fraction of the time that the sprinting ostrich's feet were on the ground that they must have exerted peak forces of 3 times body weight.

Being strong enough to run fast might not be a serious disadvantage if it were not also necessary for an ostrich's bones to be light—it is difficult and tiring to run fast in heavy boots. To power their running, ostriches have strong muscles in the thigh, at the upper end of the leg, where lightness matters least. Their feet are lightened by having shorter toes than you would expect in so large a bird, and only two toes on each foot instead of the usual four (usual, that is, for birds). In addition, their long leg bones are hollow and remarkably slender. We will find out soon how legs that are so lightly built can be sufficiently strong.

First, let us compare an ostrich leg bone with one from a close relative [PLATE 13]. The thick bone is from one of the moas, flightless birds in New Zealand that were hunted to extinction by the Maoris, probably about four hundred years ago. The thinner bone is from an ostrich leg. Moas generally have relatively thicker leg bones than ostriches, but this species is extraordinary, as its name indicates: *Pachyornis elephantopus* is derived from Greek words meaning "stout bird with elephant feet." Its feet are massive [PLATE 14].

Pachyornis stood less tall than ostriches but seems to have been considerably heavier. I have estimated its mass by making a small-scale model, taking the dimensions from a skeleton but filling in the flesh as I judged it to have been in life. I measured the volume of the model by dunking it in water, then scaled up this measurement to estimate the volume of the real bird. Finally, I calculated the mass of the moa by assuming that the density of its flesh was about the same as for modern birds. The result, about 150 kilograms (330 pounds), is a good deal more than the 100 kilograms (220 pounds) of a big male ostrich.

We will think more quantitatively about the strengths of leg bones later in this chapter, but for the present I want you to try to imagine *Pachyornis* running like an ostrich, at 16 meters per second (36 miles per hour). Did you

PLATE 13

(*above*) Ostrich tarsometatarsus (lower leg bone).
Struthio camelus
(*below*) Moa tarsometatarsus
Pachyornis elephantopus
The moas were hunted to extinction a few centuries ago. The bones of some species were very heavy, compared to the lightweight bones of ostriches.

succeed? I can't imagine it, because the power needed to swing those legs back and forward at the necessary rate seems impossibly large. The cumbersome legs of the moa will serve to emphasize the remarkably light structure of the legs of the ostrich [PLATE 12]. And many skeletons of other animals also are beautiful examples of strength with lightness [PLATE 15].

If we want to know how skeletons can best be designed for strength with lightness we should first ask what sort of material should be used. Engineers make structures and machines from four main kinds of material: metals, polymers, ceramics and composites. An ostrich with aluminum leg bones might work very well, but evolution has not mastered the art of metalworking. We will ignore the metals and think about the nature and properties of the other three kinds of material.

Polymers are built from long chains of more or less similar molecular units: rubbers and plastics are familiar examples. Rubbers consist of the small molecules of a substance called isoprene, linked together in long tangled chains. Polyethylene plastics (polythenes for short) consist of long chains of the hydrocarbon ethylene, while other plastics are built from other building blocks. Naturally occurring polymers include cellulose, which consist of chains of sugar molecules, and silk and collagen, made of linked amino acid molecules. Collagen has special interest for us because (as we will see) it is one of the principal constituents of bone.

The properties of polymers depend largely on the extent to which the individual chains of molecules are linked together. Latex, from which rubber is made, oozes from cuts made in rubber trees as a viscous liquid. Its chains of linked isoprene units are separate and can flow freely past each other. The process of vulcanization attaches sulphur atoms to the chains, bonding them together in a three-dimensional network. This converts the liquid latex to solid rubber. Rubber can be greatly stretched (to two or three times its initial length), because the initially kinked molecules unfold as it stretches, but it can only be stretched to the point at which some of the molecules are fully straightened out: beyond that, it breaks. If it is stretched and then released it recoils elastically: the molecules fold up again and it returns to its original length.

An important class of polymers is described as fibrous. Cotton and linen are plant fibers formed from the fibrous polymer cellulose. Silk is a fibrous protein produced by silkworms. The distinctive feature of these and other fibrous proteins is that instead of being tangled as in rubber their molecular chains are more neatly arranged. They may be kinked in places but for much of their length they are straight and lined up parallel to each other. The fiber

PLATE 14

Foot skeleton of an extinct moa.
Pachyornis elephantopus
A bird with feet as heavy as this is unlikely to have run fast.

PLATE 15

Skeleton of Patagonian
Mara (a rodent).
Dolichotis patagonum
The leg bones must be strong
and stiff enough to withstand the
forces of running.

cannot stretch much because the molecular chains are already nearly straight, and it is strong because the chains are tightly packed together. The fibrous polymer that concerns us most in this book is collagen, which not only is found in bone but is also the principal constituent of tendons (which attach muscles to bones) and of most ligaments (which attach bones to each other at joints). Raw tendon exists as strong white bands of collagen that can be stretched only by about 8% before breaking, but when meat is cooked the tendons swell, shorten and become transparent and rubber-like. The reason is that heating breaks down the bonds between molecules that maintain the neat, parallel array, allowing them to change from the relatively straight con-figuration found in fibers to the more folded state of rubbers.

When we consider polymers as a material for constructing bones, there are some obvious problems. Rubber is good for automobile tires but rubber-like bones would be highly unsatisfactory: imagine trying to lift a suitcase and having your rubber-like arm bones stretch while your leg bones, compressed by the load, buckled. Bones made entirely from fibrous polymers might be more serviceable, if constructed from a mesh of fibers running in different directions, but it would be hard to make them stiff enough. Similarly, no one makes bicycle frames from cotton.

Ceramics, the next group of engineering materials, are stiffer. They include stone, pottery, glass and cement. The problem with them as potential material for skeletons is that they are brittle: an ostrich with glass bones had better not stumble.

Composite materials, our final group, are mixtures of two or more simpler materials. One of the most familiar composites is fiberglass, which consists of fine fibers of glass, a ceramic, embedded in a plastic resin, a polymer. The resin is not particularly strong and would be too flexible for making boats or fishing rods. Glass by itself would be much too brittle for making either of those things. But fiberglass, made from resin and glass together, is excellent both for boats and for rods. It is stiffer and stronger than the resin by itself would be because the glass fibers reinforce it. It is much tougher (less brittle) than glass by itself would be, for reasons that need more explanation. We want to explore the question because, as we shall soon see, bone also is a composite material.

Before going further we need to be sure that we understand two words that cause endless confusion: *stress* and *strain.* Many people think of stress and strain as different words for the same thing, but the true meanings are utterly different. Stress is the force per unit area on a body that then causes it to deform: if you pull on a cord of 1 square millimeter cross section with a force of 10 newtons, the stress in the cord is 10 newtons per square millimeter. (The newton, the scientific unit of force, is approximately equal to the force exerted by gravity at sea level on a 100 gram or 3 ounce weight.) Strain is a measure of the extent to which a body is deformed when it is subject to stress: if the cord was initially 100 millimeters (4 inches) long but was stretched by the force we have been discussing to 110 millimeters (4.4 inches), its extension was 10 millimeters (.4 inch) and the strain was 10/100 = .1 (or .4/4 = .1). Stress causes strain (if you pull on a cord you will stretch it), but it is not the same thing as strain.

Two other commonly used words, *tension* and *compression,* also have specific meanings when used in describing mechanical processes. When I pull on a rope I exert tension on it, setting up tensile stresses and stretching it. When I stand on a block of rubber I compress it, setting up compressive stresses and squeezing it thinner. Fibers resist tension well but (because they are flexible) cannot resist compression: you can pull with a rope but you cannot push with it. Ceramics are apt to crack in tension but are stiff and resist compression. The tensile strength of a material is the stress needed to break it in tension, and the compressive strength is the compressive stress needed to crush it.

The tensile strength is generally found to be more or less constant for any particular material: if you double the cross-sectional area of a rope it should be able to support double the load, breaking at the same stress as the thinner rope. However, this turns out not to be true for thin strands of glass. In a remarkable series of experiments performed about 1920 the engineer A. A. Griffith found that glass rods of about 1 millimeter (.04 inch) diameter broke at stresses of about 200 newtons per square millimeter, but that fine glass fibers of diameter 3 micrometers (3/1000 millimeters or .00012 inch) could withstand 3,000 newtons per square millimeter—fifteen times the stress of the thicker rod. This means a rope made of very fine glass fibers would be much stronger than a solid rod of the same cross-sectional area.

The explanation has to do with the danger that cracks, once formed, will spread. Think of a glass rod with a crack part way across it. If forces pull on the ends of the rod, the average stress across any cross section is simply the force divided by the cross-sectional area. No force, however, can be transmitted across the crack. This means that the intact part of the cross section has to take more than its fair share of force, so it suffers larger stresses. The stresses are particularly high in the as-yet-unbroken glass very close to the crack tip, where the stress may be many times higher than the average for the entire cross-section. The stress at the crack tip may reach the tensile strength of the glass, although the average stress across the cross section is far lower.

Therefore, the crack has a serious weakening effect and is likely to grow until the bar has broken right across.

No glass or other ceramic rod is likely to have a perfectly smooth surface, especially if it has been scratched or even merely touched. Tiny cracks in the surface are almost inevitable, whether the sample is a thick rod or a thin fiber. Long cracks, however, are more dangerous than short ones: they concentrate the stress more, and if they are long enough they are liable to become unstable so that the sample will break suddenly with a bang. The advantage of fine fibers is that they cannot have long cracks in them. A 3-micrometer diameter fiber cannot have a crack running across it that is more than 3 micrometers long.

A rope of fine fibers might be stronger in tension than a solid rod, but it would be no use in compression because the fibers would buckle. The solution, if a material is needed that will take either tension or compression, is to glue the fibers together by embedding them in resin. Paradoxically, the resin must not be too strong because if it were it might carry cracks across from fiber to fiber. A relatively weak resin will split between the fibers, as a crack reaches it, stopping the crack from travelling across into the next fiber. The resins used to make fiberglass have tensile strengths of around 70 newtons per square millimeter but the strength of the fiberglass itself may be as much as 1,000 newtons per square millimeter.

Bone is a composite material like fiberglass, as also is mollusk shell [PLATE 16]. Like fiberglass, bone is stiff and reasonably strong both in tension and compression. Fiberglass has two components (glass and resin) but bone has three. They are tiny crystals of calcium phosphate (a ceramic), collagen fibers (a fibrous polymer) and a jelly-like matrix containing protein molecules with sugars bonded to them. The crystals adhere to the collagen fibers, which in turn are embedded in the matrix. With tensile strengths a little below 200 newtons per square millimeter, bone is considerably weaker than fiberglass, but it is much stronger than collagen alone would be (100 newtons per square millimeter). Also, it is less flexible than collagen fibers and, unlike them, can take compression as well as tension. Its weakness compared to fiberglass must be largely due to the ceramic being present as tiny crystals rather than long fibers.

If the collagen fibers all ran in the same direction, bone would be strong in that direction, but weak in other directions. Similarly, wood is hard to break across the grain but splits easily along the grain. In fact, bones are built up of layers with fibers running in different directions. The principle is that of plywood, which consists of thin layers of wood glued together, with the grain

PLATE 17

Tympanic bulla of a Gray's Beaked
Whale.
Mesoplodon grayi
This exceptionally brittle bone
encloses the ear ossicles.

PLATE 16

Shell of a Pearly Nautilus, cut open.
Nautilus pompilus
Like bone, mollusk shell is a
composite material. It consists of
calcium carbonate crystals cemented
together by protein.

running in different directions in successive layers. In many cases, the loads that bones have to withstand act mainly in one direction, so there is an advantage in their being stronger in that direction than in others. They must not, however, be too weak in other directions. Spruce wood, with all its fibers running along the grain, is thirty times weaker when stretched across the grain as when stretched along the grain. Bone from cow legs, with fibers running in several directions, is only three times weaker across than along the grain.

Designers of fiberglass structures try to arrange the fibers in the most advantageous way and may set more fibers in one direction than in others to suit the anticipated pattern of forces, but bone seems to be designed in a more complicated and subtle way. Concentric layers of fibers wrap round the outside of a bone [FIGURE B] and also, on a smaller scale, concentric layers wrap around blood vessels that run along the length of the bone. The fibers run in different directions in successive layers, often alternating between left-handed helices (corkscrew curves) in one layer and right-handed ones in the next, but the angles of the helices may be different in different parts of the bone, apparently to suit the different stresses to which they are likely to be exposed. Where tension has to be resisted the fibers run more nearly lengthwise along the bone but where compression has to be resisted they run in flatter coils that bind the bone together, reinforcing it against bursting under load. Some layers have a higher proportion of collagen fibers, good for resisting tension, while others have more crystals, good against compression.

There are different kinds of bone with different material properties. Similarly, different kinds of wood have different properties: spruce is soft and splits easily, teak is hard and strong, and balsa is very light. John Currey of York University, England, set out to discover whether bones that serve different functions are made of different kinds of bone with suitably different properties. He selected three bones for comparison. The first was the femur (thigh bone) of a cow, which John selected as an ordinary sort of bone, subject during the life of the animal to the moderately rough sort of treatment that most bones have to endure. The other two he chose as extreme cases. The tympanic bone of a whale, part of the ear, is buried deep in the head [PLATE 17]. Its function does not require it to withstand any large forces and in its position, deep below the blubber, it is very well protected from knocks. By contrast, taking knocks is a large part of the function of antlers of stags, the third chosen group of bones [PLATE 18]. Antlers are used in fights between males to decide the right to breed with groups of females. Rival stags clash antlers and wrestle until the weaker gives way.

A material like porcelain would seem quite suitable for making tympanic

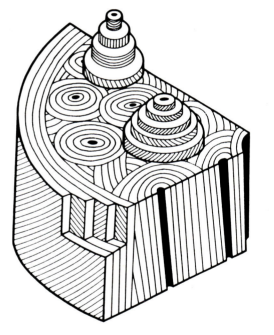

FIGURE B

This greatly-enlarged diagram shows the structure of a block cut from a bone. Concentric layers of bone lie parallel to the outer surface or enclose the blood vessels within the bone. The collagen fibers run in different directions, in successive layers.

bones but would be disastrous for antlers, which would shatter in the first fight. To decide what kind of material would be good for antlers, we will think a little about breaking crockery. Whether a porcelain cup is broken by a fall depends on the energy involved. A cup dropped from a height of one meter is falling faster when it hits the floor, with twice as much kinetic energy, as if it were dropped from half a meter. At impact the cup is brought to a halt and deformed elastically (yes, even china cups have elastic properties). Its kinetic energy is converted to elastic strain energy which is momentarily stored in the deformed cup. If all is well, the stresses in the cup do not rise too high and it bounces: the elastic energy is converted back to kinetic energy in the elastic recoil. However, if the kinetic energy of the falling cup is greater than the elastic energy that can be stored in it, the stresses in the cup reach either the tensile or the compressive strength of the material and the cup breaks. A cup dropped from one meter may have enough energy to shatter; if dropped from half a meter it might bounce unharmed.

When I was at school we drank out of glass tumblers, which often broke. Some "unbreakable" plastic tumblers were bought as replacements, and a master set some of us to finding out whether they really were unbreakable. We threw them against a wall and jumped on them and eventually broke a few, but it was difficult. The important difference between the plastic tumblers and the glass ones was that the plastic ones were more flexible. They could deform a lot before breaking, storing up more elastic strain energy than the rigid glass tumblers. A material like the plastic of those tumblers, that needs a lot of energy to break it, is described by engineers as tough. In contrast, a brittle material like glass needs little energy to break it.

To find out how tough the femur, tympanic bone and antler were, John Currey cut samples from the three bones and tested them in a machine of the kind that engineers use for testing samples of metals and plastics. He found that the whale tympanic bulla was very weak. It was also very stiff, so a very little energy was enough to break it: it was brittle. The femur of the cow and the antler of the stag were both much stronger (with the femur just a little stronger than the antler) but the antler was almost twice as flexible as the femur, so could store more elastic energy. Thus the antler was made of tough bone, the femur of bone with intermediate properties and the bulla of brittle bone.

This tells us that, as suits their functions, antler is very good at taking knocks, bulla very bad and femur middling. The reason for the difference emerged when the bones were analyzed. The ceramic calcium phosphate and other minerals in the bone make up 59% of the mass of antler, 67% of cow

femur and 86% of whale bulla. A high proportion of calcium phosphate makes bone stiffer, and if the proportion rises too high the bone becomes weaker because the benefits of being a composite (fiberglass-like) material are partially lost.

Old people often break bones in falls that would not bother children. The reason for the weakness of our old bones is partly that they become porous, but largely that the proportion of calcium phosphate increases: young children's bones have a mineral content of about 61%, little more than antler, but those of middle-aged people contain about 66% minerals. John Currey tested bone from people who had died at ages ranging from three to ninety and found that samples from the oldest bones needed three times less energy to break them than did equal-sized samples from the children.

Buffaloes clash horns much as stags clash antlers, but are protected from damage in a different way. The horns have a core of bone but, unlike antlers, are covered by a thick sheath of horn [PLATE 19]. No one has tested the bone of the core, but there is no reason to suppose that its properties are unusual. The horn, which is made of a fingernail-like material, cushions the bone against the impacts, and much of the energy involved must be stored as elastic energy in the horn.

We have examined the properties of bone as a material, seeing how it can be made strong and resistant to impacts. Now we will think about bones as structures. How should they be formed to be strong and yet light?

The answer depends on the patterns of force that they will have to withstand. If forces pull lengthwise on the ends of a bone, the whole bone is in tension. It will not matter what shape the bone is in cross section (whether it is round or triangular, whether it is a solid rod or a hollow tube): all that will matter is whether it has a large enough cross-sectional area to keep the stress (force divided by area) below the tensile strength of bone. If forces push lengthwise on the ends of the bone, loading it in compression, the situation is more complicated: not only must the cross-sectional area be enough to keep the stresses below the compressive strength, so that the bone is not crushed, but the bone must be stiff enough not to buckle like an empty beer can. One way to make it stiff but light would be to form it as a hollow tube, and bicycle frames are built from hollow tubes for precisely that reason. A bicycle with a frame of solid rods would have to be intolerably heavy, to be stiff enough. Similarly, most long bones are hollow tubes, which is why they are suitable for making flutes [PLATE 5].

If you want to break a stick or any other long, slender object you will probably not apply tension or compression along its length. Instead you will bend

PLATE 18

Skull and antlers of a male Fallow Deer.
Dama dama
Antler is a tough material that withstands impacts well.

it by applying forces at right angles to its length. A rod bent into a curve is longer along the outside of the curve than along the inside. This tells us that bending stretches one side of the rod and compresses the other, setting up tensile stresses on one side and compressive stresses on the other. The rod will break if the highest tensile stress (at the surface of the rod, on the outside of the bend) reaches the tensile strength or if the highest compressive stress (at the surface on the inside of the bend) reaches the compressive strength.

Bending of a solid rod is resisted by the material on the outside of the bend (which is in tension) and on the inside of the bend (in compression). The core of this rod serves little useful function so we can eliminate it, creating a hollow tube instead of a rod, with very little effect on strength or stiffness. We can make the hollow tube fully as strong and stiff as the solid rod by increasing its diameter just a little, and it will still be lighter than the rod. The tubular structure of bones and bicycle frames gives strength with lightness in bending, as well as providing the stiffness that protects against buckling in compression.

Biologists have used a technique taken from engineering to find out about the stresses that act in the bones of living animals in activities such as running and jumping. In their simplest form, strain gauges are strips of metal foil on a paper or plastic backing, with wires attached to the ends of the foil. Engineers glue strain gauges to the surfaces of girders and other structures that they want to test, so that when forces are applied, the gauge will be stretched if the structure stretches and compressed if it is compressed. This changes the electrical resistance of the foil, which can be detected if the wires are connected to a suitable instrument. Records obtained in this way indicate strain (deformation) rather than stress (force per unit area), but if the properties of the material are known the stress can be calculated.

Engineers use strain gauges to discover the stresses in girders, but biologists have used them to discover stresses in bones. Tiny strain gauges can be glued to the surfaces of a bone in a simple surgical operation. This has been done in experiments with sheep, horses, geese and various other animals, and also with a human volunteer who allowed a strain gauge to be glued to his tibia (shin bone) and apparently suffered no ill effects. (He was a member of the team of scientists conducting the investigation and presumably thought the scientific glory compensated for a little physical inconvenience.) Until the experiment is complete, the wires are left protruding through the skin so that strains can be recorded as the animal runs, jumps or even (in the case of the goose) flies.

If a bone were purely in tension, tensile strain would be recorded from all its surfaces; if it were in compression, there would be compressive strain on all

PLATE 19

Skull and horns of African Buffalo.
Synceros caffer
The black horn contrasts with the white bones of the skull. It helps to cushion impacts, in fights between rival males.

5147.

5147

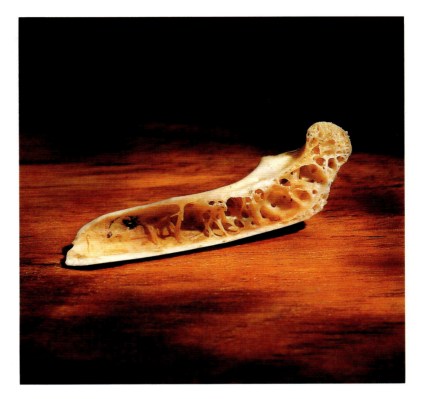

PLATE 21

Bird femur (thigh bone).
This bone has been cut open to show
its thin wall, and the reinforcing struts
of bone inside.

PLATE 20

A fossil pterosaur.
Pterodactylus elegans (Jurassic period,
about 150 million years ago).
Like many birds, pterosaurs had bones
filled with air instead of marrow.

its surfaces; and if it were being bent there would be tensile strain on one face and compressive strain on the opposite face. So far, experiments with strain gauges have discovered only two bones that are regularly in tension, in normal use. They are the humerus and ulna (both arm bones) of a gibbon, and are in tension as the ape swings by its arms through the trees. Other limb bones suffer combinations of compression and bending: when used in locomotion they have compressive strain on one side of the bone and either tensile strain or a smaller compressive strain on the other. Usually, there is compressive strain on one side and tensile on the other, indicating that bending is the predominant form of applied stress, which is why nearly all bones can be expected to benefit from tubular structure.

That leaves open the question, is it better to have a fairly narrow, thick-walled tube or a thinner-walled tube of larger diameter? We will get different answers for bones whose cavities are empty, filled only with air, and for bones that are filled with marrow.

Many of the long bones of birds are filled with air (the cavities inside them are connected to the lungs). The extinct pterosaurs [PLATE 20] also had air-filled bones. To be as light as possible for their strength, such bones should have thin walls and large diameters. The larger the diameter the better, because the farther apart the tension and compression surfaces are, the more leverage they have to resist bending. The fuselage of an airplane is a good example of a large-diameter, thin-walled tube. However, the wall of a tube should not be so thin, in comparison to the diameter, as to be liable to fail by buckling. Bend a plastic drinking straw and it will probably not break cleanly across, but its cross section will flatten at the bend until, suddenly, it gives way by buckling. Bones should not be so thin-walled as to be liable to fail like that. Air-filled bones of birds and pterosaurs generally have walls that are thin, but not excessively so [PLATE 21]. The thickness of the wall is often 6-20% of the radius of the bone shaft, implying that the diameter of the cavity is 80-94% of the diameter of the bone.

Other bird bones, and mammal bones, are filled not with air but with fatty yellow marrow. This kind of marrow seems not to be much use; the fat does not get used for metabolism, even when the animal is starving. There is another kind of marrow which is red because it forms blood cells; it is found in young bones, but in adults mainly in the bones of the skull and spine. This red marrow is intensely useful to the animal but the yellow marrow in adult long bones seems to be just so much dead weight. The mass of the marrow has to be considered, as well as the mass of bone, in comparing the merits of thick- and thin-walled tubular bones.

Consider a tubular bone that has to be strong enough to do a particular job. We have already seen that the thinner its wall, in comparison to its diameter, the less bone is needed. The thinner the wall and the larger the diameter, however, the more marrow is needed to fill the central cavity. The total mass is the mass of bone plus the mass of marrow, and it turns out that this is least when the diameter of the marrow cavity is about 60% of the diameter of the bone. Some marrow-filled bones have relatively thicker and some relatively thinner walls, but nearly all are thicker-walled than air-filled bones [PLATE 22] and the most common proportions are close to those suggested by theory, with the cavity about 60% of the bone's outside diameter.

Some exceptional mammals have solid long bones. They include manatees, which look superficially like seals but are not closely related to them and feed on water plants rather than fish. What we have said so far suggests that their long bones, being solid, are needlessly heavy. Also, they have ribs that seem unnecessarily thick [PLATE 23]. It seems possible that their heavy bones are useful ballast, making diving easier by counteracting some of the buoyancy of the lungs.

Tubular construction is generally good for long bones. Plate-like bones, such as those in a sloth's pelvic girdle [PLATE 24], have to be constructed differently. Shoulder blades and many skull bones are also plate like. I want the bones of my skull roof to be fairly stiff, so that they are not easily dented by a blow. The bending accompanying a blow stretches one surface of a plate and compresses the other, so bone near the surfaces is most effective for stiffening. Many plate-like bones, such as the roof of the human skull [PLATE 25], are made stiff but light by being formed of two layers of compact bone, with spongy bone sandwiched between. Similar structures are also used in packaging and engineering. Boxes are often made of corrugated cardboard sandwiched between two flat sheets. Lightweight metal panels are constructed on the same principle.

Spongy bone (also called cancellous bone) is a three-dimensional network of bony struts, rather like a bath sponge made of bone. By itself it would be much weaker than compact bone. Spongy bone that has half its volume marrow and the other half bone is only one quarter as strong as an equal-sized piece of compact bone. A bone that was spongy throughout would be weak. But functioning as a spacer, keeping the layers of compact bone apart, spongy bone gives the skull roof the stiffness needed to prevent denting, while leaving it reasonably light. It also gives the pelvic girdles of sloths [PLATE 24] the strength needed to resist the pull of the big leg muscles that attach to them, without making them too heavy.

PLATE 22

Two thick-walled mammal bones
(*center* and *right*) contrasted with a
much thinner-walled bone from
a bird (*left*).

PLATE 23

Ribs of a Caribbean Manatee.
Trichechus manatus
These heavy, solid bones may
function as ballast.

PLATE 24

Pelvis of Pale-throated Sloth.
Bradypus tridactylus
The broad plates provide attachment
areas for hip muscles.

PLATE 25

The roof of a human skull.
Homo sapiens
The cut edge where the skull roof
has been sawn off shows its sandwich
structure.

PLATE 27

Mastodon skull.
Mammut americanus (extinct since
about 10,000 years ago)
Spare space is filled by a lightweight
honeycomb of bone.

PLATE 26

The inside of the shell of a
Painted Turtle.
Chrysemys picta
The vertebrae are attached to the
strong shell, so they can be more
slender than in other similar-sized
reptiles.

The protective shells of turtles are built of bony plates, with spongy bone sandwiched between compact bone, and a layer of horn on the outer surface. The stiffness of the shell makes the backbone redundant, and the vertebrae are reduced to rudiments attached to the inner surface of the shell [PLATE 26].

As well as forming a spacer layer in bony plates of sandwich construction, spongy bone fills the heads of long bones, where they meet other bones at joints [PLATE 21]. It also fills the inside of vertebrae. In every case, however, it is covered by a layer of compact bone.

It is surely no surprise to find light construction in the skeletons of fast-running ostriches or of flying birds and pterosaurs. Less expected, perhaps, are marvels of lightweight design in the skulls of elephants and the necks of dinosaurs. Elephants have relatively small brains, far too small to fill their big skulls. The surplus space between the brain and the outer surface of the skull is filled with a delicate honeycomb of thin sheets of bone, an extreme case of sandwich construction [PLATE 27]. We will discuss in Chapter 8 why elephants and other large animals have relatively small brains.

Apatosaurus, commonly called the brontosaur, was one of the largest land animals that ever lived. It was about 21 meters (70 feet) long, almost as long as a tennis court (23.8 meters/78 feet). No one has had the opportunity to weigh one, but measurements on scale models show that the mass of the living animal must have been about 35 tons, as much as seven large male African elephants. One of the vertebrae from its long neck [PLATE 28] shows a framework of remarkably slender bars of bone. If the backbone had not been solidly built, the dinosaur's neck would have been even heavier.

Some bones are exceedingly delicate and others remarkably heavy. For an example of delicate bones, look up the nose of any mammal skull, such as the skull of the sea otter [PLATE 29]. Look at the scrolls of bone which support the soft tissues that warm and moisten the air breathed in. They are protected from damage by the bones of the snout, and need only be stiff enough not to collapse. For examples of heavy bones, look at the moa's legs [PLATE 13] or (if you can find a specimen of this rare animal) at the extraordinary vertebrae of the hero shrew. This small African mammal, about the size of a hamster, has a back so strong that full-grown men have stood on it, apparently without causing injury.

Such extremes of delicacy and strength raise the question, how strong should bones be? The obvious answer is that they should be strong enough not to break, but bones do break [PLATE 30]. Counts of bones of American Indians in an ancient cemetery in Ohio showed that 3% of the bones had healed fractures. (Only healed fractures were counted to avoid counting bones

PLATE 28

Sixth neck vertebra of a brontosaur.
Apatosaurus (Jurassic period, about
140 million years ago)
The openwork structure saves weight,
making the long neck easier to
support.

PLATE 30

Fossil horse rib.
Epihippus (Miocene period, 5-24
million years ago)
This bone shows a badly-healed
fracture.

PLATE 29

Sea Otter skull.
Enhydra lutris
This view up the nostrils shows the
delicate scrolls of bone in the nose.

that might have been broken after death.) Similarly, 2% of long bones showed healed fractures in a collection of gibbon skeletons and .3% in a collection of gull skeletons. Bones are clearly not strong enough to withstand all possible accidents, and would be intolerably heavy if they were.

A comparison with engineering may help us to understand the principles that presumably guide the evolution of bone strength. Suppose an engineer were commissioned to design a bridge that was expected to have to carry a maximum load of 100 tons. An optimist might calculate the thickness of beams that would just support 100 tons, and make the beams that thick. He or she might get away with it, but there is a severe danger that the bridge would fail because of two uncertainties. First, you can never be sure that a bridge will be as strong as it was designed to be, because of variations in the quality of successive batches of steel and because of possible faults in workmanship (a misplaced hole for a bolt, perhaps). Secondly, you can never be sure of your prediction of maximum load. (Several overloaded trucks may cross simultaneously.) For these reasons, an engineer designing a bridge expected to have to carry 100 tons might aim to make it strong enough to take 200 tons, giving it a factor of safety of two.

Evolution seems to have done something like that—or evolution together with the adjustments that the body makes to match the strengths of bones to the forces they experience. (X-ray pictures show that the forearm bones of a professional tennis player are much thicker in the arm that holds the racquet than in the other.) Strain gauges fitted to leg bones of horses indicated tensile stresses up to half the tensile strength of bone, and compressive stresses up to half the compressive strength, when the animals went over small jumps. Similar stresses were found in the humerus (upper arm bone), in the wing of a flying goose. These and other records indicate that bones are often two to five times as strong as is necessary for normal strenuous activities: they have safety factors between two and five.

So far as I know, no one has put strain gauges on ostrich bones, but I have estimated the stresses in fast running by analyzing films and measuring leg bones. The safety factor of the tibia (shin bone) seems to be about 2.5. No scientist ever saw a moa run but I estimate that if it ran like an ostrich, the safety factor of its tibia also would be 2.5. However, I cannot believe that it ran so fast on those heavy legs and conclude that its safety factor was much higher. If I am right, why should moas have higher safety factors than ostriches?

A cynical engineer might choose the safety factor for a bridge by adding up two costs: the cost of construction and the cost of insuring against the bridge collapsing. A very strong bridge would be very expensive to build and a very weak one would be prohibitively expensive to insure, but there would be an intermediate strength for which the total cost of construction and insurance would be least. Our engineer would design his or her bridge to have that strength.

The best safety factor for a bridge, by this criterion, would depend on the cost of materials and the degree of uncertainty over maximum loads. If platinum were the only building material available, we would make bridges weaker and live more dangerously. If strict policing made overloaded trucks very unlikely, we might again be willing to make bridges weaker.

Such considerations may explain the apparent difference of safety factor, between ostrich and moa bones. For them, however, the main cost of strength is probably not the cost of materials. The effect of heavy bones on running ability may be more important: strong, heavy bones are cumbersome and would slow the bird down. Ostriches are in danger from lions and other predators from which they escape by running, so for them heavy leg bones might be fatal. The moas, however, lived in New Zealand where there were no large predators until humans arrived, a few centuries before their extinction. For them, extra leg strength came cheaply, so the optimum safety factor may have been higher for them than for ostriches. If steel were very cheap we would build our bridges even stronger, making them ultra-safe.

In this long chapter we have seen how the nature of bone as a composite material makes for strength with lightness, as do the tubular structure of long bones and the sandwich structure of bony plates. We have seen why bones that have to take knocks, as antlers do, should be more flexible than bones in less exposed positions need to be. And, we have seen that the best safety factors for different bones may differ according to their circumstances: there may have been a good reason for moas to have had such astonishingly thick bones.

Chapter 3

JOINTS

_____

JOINTS are generally needed between bones, to allow movements: if I did not have an elbow joint, I could not bend my arm. This chapter is about the many kinds of joints and the movements they allow. We will examine joints in the backs of fishes, the jaws of lions and the legs of horses. We will see how most joints are lubricated, and how their surfaces are shaped to allow some movements and prevent others. First, however, we will look at an example of a bone that is flexible enough to allow considerable movement without having a joint.

This is the wishbone of a bird [PLATE 31]. Its flexibility is obvious when you handle the wishbone of a freshly roasted fowl, but the discovery that it bends in flight came from a remarkable experiment by Farish Jenkins and his colleagues at Harvard University, who made an X-ray film of a flying starling. They might have tried to capture the bird on film as it flew past their X-ray machine but they made their task easier by training it to fly against the jet of air in a wind-tunnel. The trained bird matched its speed to the wind, remaining stationary in the laboratory, so they were able to keep it flying in the field of the camera. Not surprisingly, the images in the film are rather fuzzy, but they give the amazing impression of a flying skeleton. They show that the arms of the wishbone were 19 millimeters (.75 inches) apart at the top of the upstroke but only 13 millimeters (.5 inches) apart at the bottom of the

PLATE 31

Wishbone of an eagle (species unknown).
Most movement in skeletons occurs at joints, but the wishbone of birds bends and recoils at every wing beat.

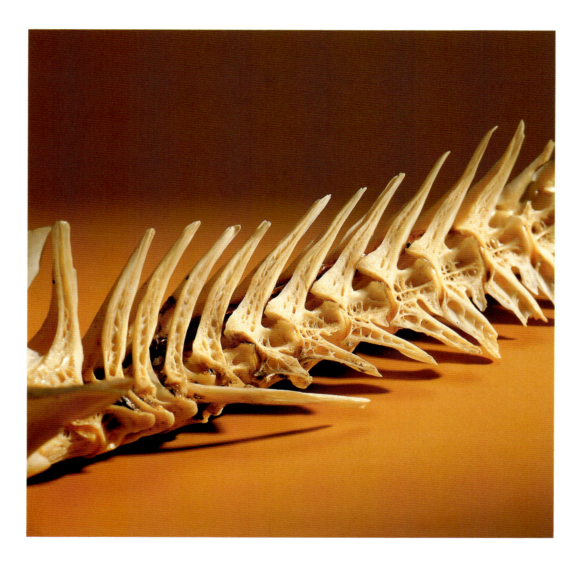

PLATE 32

Backbone of an Atlantic Cod.
Gadus morhua
Successive vertebrae are connected
by pads of flexible tissue.

PLATE 33

Backbone of a Nine-banded
Armadillo.
Dasypus novemcinctus
The skeleton is lying on its back
with the pelvis to the left of the
picture and the shoulder region to the
right. The vertebrae interlock in ways
that allow some movements and
prevent others.

PLATE 35

Vertebrae of a Lion's back.
Panthera leo
The back bends and extends in
each galloping stride.

downstroke. The arms of the wishbone bent in and splayed out again, as the wings beat up and down.

Such flexible bones are exceptional. Most movements of vertebrate animals depend on joints that allow more or less rigid bones to move relative to each other. Look at a fish backbone [PLATE 32]. Each vertebra is a spool-shaped lump of bone with spines above and supports for the bases of the ribs projecting from their sides. In the living animal, each spool-shaped vertebral body is connected to the next by a pad of flexible tissue which allows the vertebral column to bend from side to side as the fish swims.

Look at the vertebrae from the lumbar region (the lower back) of an armadillo [PLATE 33]. As in fish, there are flexible pads between vertebrae. These are the intervertebral discs in humans which are responsible for a great deal of backache. Each disc is fibrous outside and jellylike in the middle. In the complaint known as a slipped disc, some of the jelly squirts out. This sometimes happens, because the discs have to take very large loads—for example, 8,000 newtons (almost 2,000 pounds force) in a young man bending over to lift a heavy weight.

The backs of armadillos are protected by bony plates, arranged rather like the armor of medieval knights [PLATE 34]. When danger threatens, some species of armadillo roll up to form (in the case of the Three-banded Armadillo of Argentina) a near-perfect sphere, completely enclosed by the armor. To make this possible, the joints between the lumbar vertebrae must be free to bend up and down. Other movements that the flexible discs might

PLATE 34

The hide of a Nine-banded Armadillo.
Dasypus novemcinctus
This flexible armor consists of bony
plates embedded in the skin.

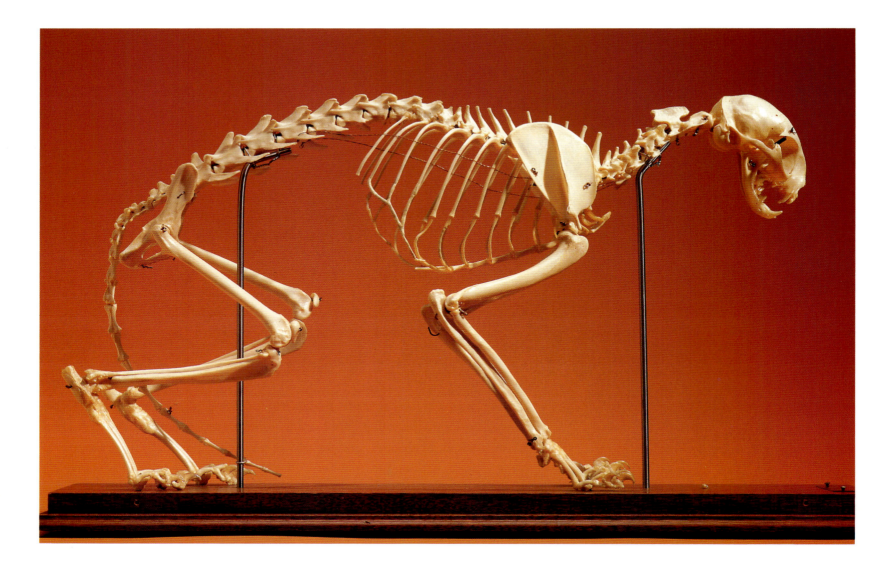

Skeleton of a domestic cat.
Felis catus
Different parts of the backbone can
bend and twist in different ways.

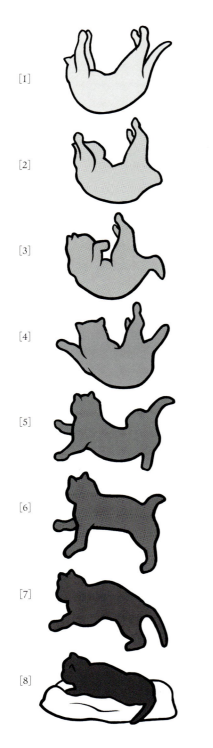

A cat dropped upside-down can right itself before landing. This sequence of drawings is based on a film.

allow are restricted by interlocking projections (known as zygapophyses) on successive vertebrae. A pair of outward-facing zygapophyses on the rear of each vertebra fits between a pair of inward-facing ones on the front of the next vertebra behind. The vertical surfaces of the zygapophyses, which rub together, are covered in the living animal by a smooth layer of cartilage and bathed in lubricating fluid, just like the leg joints that will be described soon. Because of the way they are angled, the armadillo zygapophyses allow the up-and-down bending that is needed for rolling up but prevent side-to-side bending, and also twisting.

Few mammals roll up like armadillos, but most gallop. In galloping, the back bends strongly at one stage of the stride to bring the hind legs forward, and straightens again as these legs swing back. In other mammals as in armadillos, the lumbar vertebrae are jointed so as to allow up-and-down bending [PLATE 35].

Different parts of the vertebral columns of mammals have their zyga-pophyses arranged in different ways, allowing different possibilities for movement. This is illustrated by an experiment with domestic cats [PLATE 36]. If a cat is dropped upside-down, it can usually right itself in the air and land on its feet. (Please don't try this in case something goes wrong and your pet gets hurt.) The movements involved [FIGURE C] can be sequenced. With its back arched [stage 2] the cat twists the fore part of its body round to one side [4]. It then straightens its back and reverses the twist [6]. Quite complicated arguments involving the principle of conservation of angular momentum are needed to explain why this maneuver gets the cat right way up.

Vertebrae are connected by flexible discs which distort as the joints move. In contrast, in leg joints bones press directly on each other, and their surfaces slide over each other as the joint moves. An example is the horse fetlock [PLATE 37]. Horses have just one toe on each foot and run on tiptoe (the hoof is equivalent to a fingernail). The fetlock joint corresponds to the joint where the base of your middle finger meets the connecting bone in the palm of your hand. In a horse it is a hinge joint, allowing bending but no other movement. It is held together by a ligament (a band of collagen fibers) on each side, with the bottom end of the cannon bone fitting neatly in the hollow in the top of the toe bone. The joint could bend just as well if the end of the cannon bone were shaped like a cylinder halved lengthwise, and the end of the toe bone a corresponding cylindrical hollow. However, a cylinder in a cylindrical hollow not only can rotate, but also can slide along its own axis. A horse does not want its toes to be free to slide sideways off its foot. The end of the cannon bone is not simply cylindrical but has a projecting flange that fits a groove in

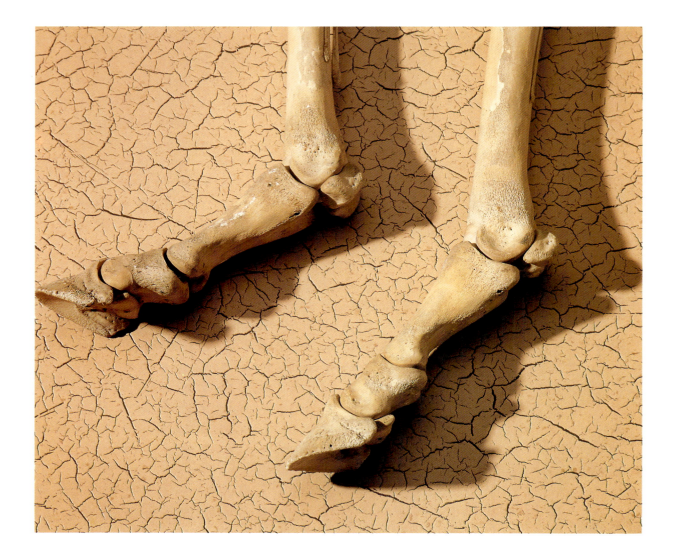

PLATE 37

Skeletons of horse feet.
Equus caballus
The fetlock joints are bent to
different angles. They are bent
forwards as in these pictures when the
hoof is on the ground but bend
backwards while the foot is swinging
forward for the next step.

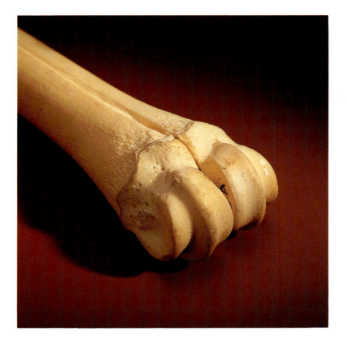

the hollow in the toe bone. This prevents the toes from sliding off sideways,
much as the flanges on the wheels of railway trains prevent them from slipping off the rails. Similar flanged joint surfaces are found in deer, which, however, have two toes jointed to the single cannon bone [PLATE 38].

At this point we need to think about the types of movements that joints
allow. The hinged horse toe joint allows rotation about its axis, but no other
movement. Think of a door hinged to its frame. The only movement it can
make is rotation about the hinge axis, opening and closing. The door's position can be described by stating just one quantity. I may say that the free edge
of the door is 50 centimeters (20 inches) from the jamb, or that the door is at
an angle of 30° to the wall—these two statements are alternatives that give the
same information. Therefore, we say that a hinge joint allows just one degree
of freedom of movement between the bodies that it connects.

Not all joint movements are rotations. Another class of joints allows one
structure to slide forward and back on another. There is a joint like this in the
back of the clawed toad, an amphibian that uses its big hind legs for swimming breaststroke. The pelvis can slide forward and back on the backbone,
like a drawer sliding in and out of a desk. It slides back in the power stroke of
swimming, giving an extra push to the water. The position of a simple sliding
joint can be described by just one measurement (for example, the distance an

PLATE 39

Lion skull.
Panthera leo
The skull has been laid upside
down to show the grooves for the
jaw joints.

open drawer protrudes from the front of the desk) so again we have just one degree of freedom.

Many joints allow more than one degree of freedom. We saw that the fetlock joint of a horse was a hinge allowing just one degree of freedom. Now try the corresponding joint in your own body, the joint where your middle finger meets the palm of your hand [PLATE 40]. You can bend and extend this joint, as when you close and open your fist. You can also waggle the finger from side to side in the plane of your hand, as when you spread your fingers and bring them together again. To describe the position of the joint you have to give angles for both these kinds of movement, so there are two degrees of freedom. The side-to-side movement is possible because instead of a flanged cylindrical end like that of the horse, the metacarpal bone (the bone in your palm, equivalent to the horse's cannon bone) has a simpler-shaped end, rounded like half an egg. The equivalent in engineering is a universal joint, as in the drive train of automobiles, which also allows two degrees of freedom of rotation.

Other joints allow combinations of rotation and sliding. The skull of a lion [PLATE 39] has two parts, the main body of the skull and the lower jaw. The left and right jaw joints each consist of a rod of bone attached to the lower jaw resting in a close-fitting groove in the skull. It allows the jaw to open and close and also slide from side to side—two degrees of freedom.

PLATE 40

Skeleton of a human hand.
Homo sapiens
There are universal joints at the
bases of the fingers.

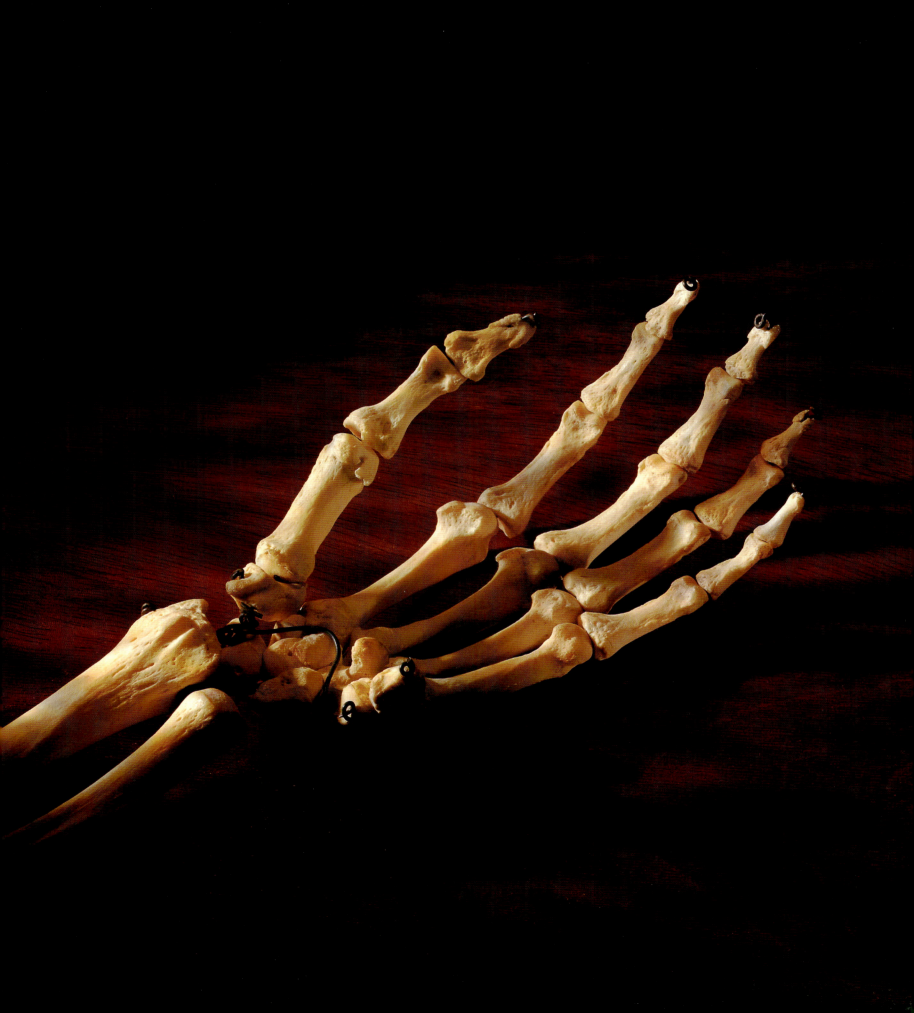

PLATE 41

Skull of a capybara.
Hydrochaeris hydrochaeris
The capybara, from South America, is
the largest of all rodents. The grooves
for the jaw joints (a little behind and
to the sides of the back teeth) run
forward and back, not transversely
across the skull as in the lion.

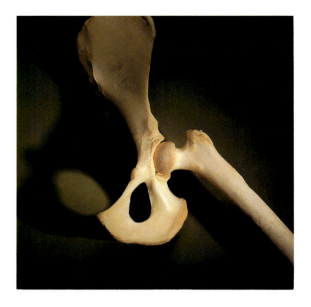

PLATE 42

Hip joint of an Orangutan.
Pongo pygmaeus
A ball on the head of the femur
(thigh bone) fits a socket in
the pelvis.

The sliding movement is important because cats have big blade-like back teeth, which they use for slicing through flesh. The upper and lower teeth work together like the blades of scissors. The lower jaw is narrower than the upper, so when the lion closes its mouth its lower teeth lie some distance from its upper ones. When, however, meat is to be cut on (say) the left side of the mouth, the jaw is moved over to the left so that the upper and lower cutting teeth of that side make close contact, like the blades of a well-made pair of scissors.

Many animals (but not cats) can slide their jaws forward and back. When you want to bring your front teeth together edge to edge to bite through a cookie, you have to move your lower jaw forward. If you then want to chew the cookie between your back teeth, you must move your jaw back. In the forward position your back teeth cannot meet and in the backward one your front teeth do not meet, so you have to move the jaw forward and back for the various processes of eating. You also, of course, need to be able to open and close your mouth, which requires a second degree of freedom, and the side-to-side movements of chewing use a third. Rodents chew by forward-and-back movements so do not need this third degree of freedom but have a nicely constructed jaw joint to allow the other two [PLATE 41]. Rounded knobs on the lower jaw rest in grooves that run forward and back in the skull, and can rock or slide in the grooves.

For another example of a joint that allows three degrees of freedom of movement, look at the hip joint of an ape [PLATE 42]. A spherical knob on

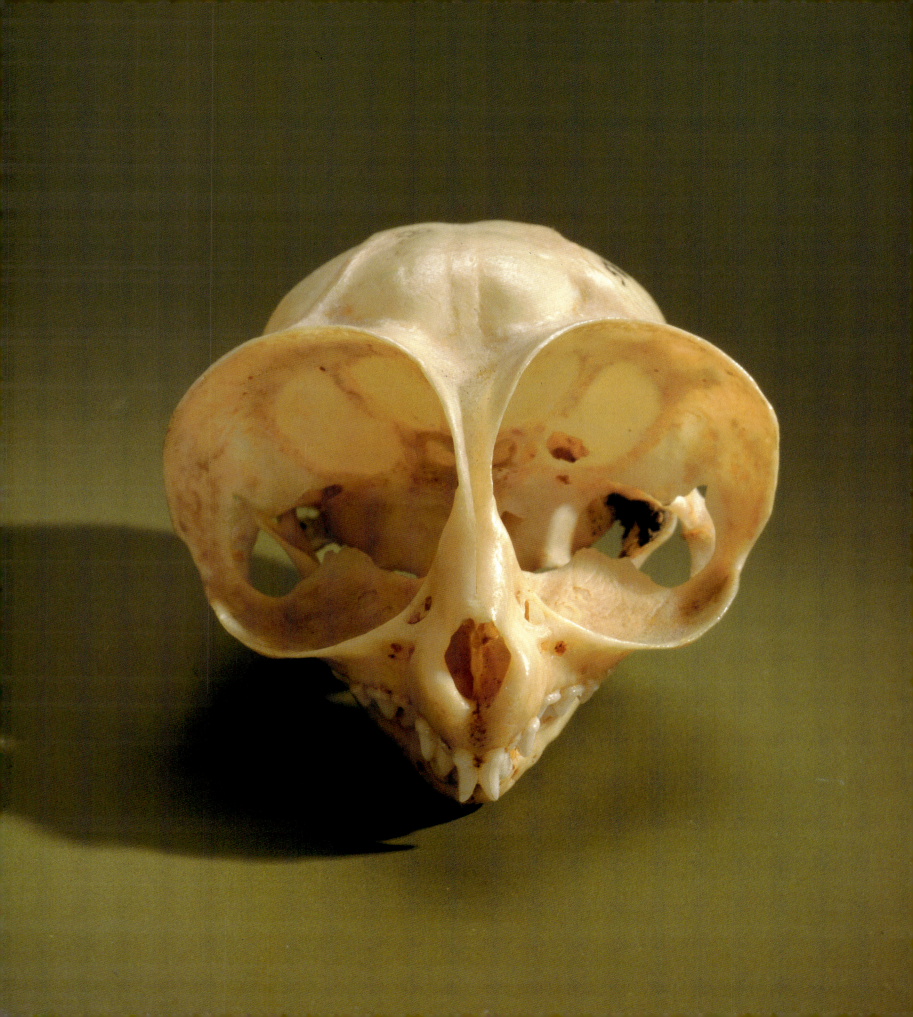

PLATE 44

Human foot.
Homo sapiens
A joint within the foot allows the
sole to rock from side to side.
The foot is lying sole-upward with
the calcaneus (heel bone) on the right
and the talus partly hidden under it.

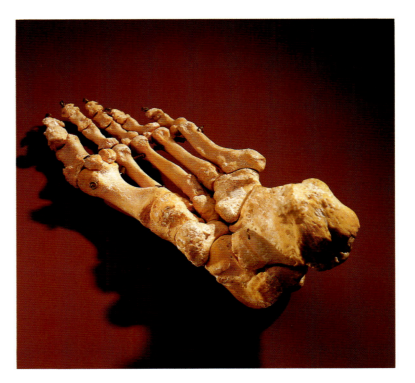

PLATE 43

Skull of a Sulawesi Tarsier.
Tarsius spectrum
This South-East Asian relative of
monkeys and lemurs is active mainly
at night. The huge eyes (good for
night vision) can turn freely in
their sockets.

the top end of the femur fits into a cup-shaped socket in the pelvic girdle. Ball-and-socket joints like this are also used in engineering, for example to mount rear-view mirrors in vehicles, so that they can be tilted to suit every driver. Such joints allow rotation about any axis through the center of the ball but are described as allowing just three degrees of freedom. To understand why, try the movements of your own hip, which is also a ball and socket. Keeping your knee straight and moving only the hip joint, you can swing your leg forward and back; or you can swing it out to your side; or you can rotate the leg about its own long axis so that the toes point forward or sideways. Any movement that the hip allows can be described as a combination of those three rotations, so we have three degrees of freedom.

The eye is another case of a ball in a socket [PLATE 43]. I can turn my eyes from side to side or tilt them up and down as I look around, but I do not seem to be able to make them rotate clockwise and counterclockwise, as seen from in front. This has nothing to do with the form of the ball and socket, but is simply because of my inability to coordinate my muscles in the required way. Here is a joint that in principle allows three degrees of freedom, but only two of them are used.

Many movements depend not on a single joint, but on two or more. To try an example, lift up your foot and wiggle it around. You will find you can tilt your foot toe-up and toe-down, or you can turn the sole of your foot inwards in the movement called supination, or outwards (pronation). This may give you the impression that your ankle is a single joint with two degrees of freedom, like the joint at the base of your finger, but it is actually two distinct hinge joints set at an angle to each other. The clue to understanding it is a pair of interlocking bones [PLATE 44], the talus and calcaneus. These form a fairly rigid unit, between the two hinges. The upward projection on the talus, shaped like a half-cylinder, fits into a hollow in the lower end of the tibia, forming the hinge that allows us to tilt our feet toe-up and toe-down. The front ends of the talus and calcaneus articulate with the bones further forward in the foot to form the second hinge, which allows pronation and supination. In these movements, the front part of the foot moves relative to the talus and calcaneus much as your hands move relative to each other when you twist a wet cloth to wring out the water.

Let us think about the number of leg joints a monkey might like to have, to be able to grasp with its foot any branch within reach, whatever the angle of the branch [PLATE 45]. It needs to be able to move its foot in three directions (up and down, forward and back, side to side) and also to be able to rotate it about three axes. In all, it needs six degrees of freedom. Like us, it

PLATE 45

Skeleton of a White-throated Capuchin Monkey hindleg.
Cebus capucinus
The leg joints allow the foot to be placed in different positions and at different angles.

PLATE 46

Asiatic Mouse Deer skeleton.
Tragulus javanicus
Mammals stand with their feet close
in under the body.

PLATE 47

Skeleton of an iguana lizard.
Iguana iguana
Reptiles sprawl with their feet
well to the side of the body.

has three degrees of freedom in the hip, one in the knee (a hinge) and two in the ankle, precisely the six that are needed.

I have been ignoring the obvious fact that our joints have to be shaped to allow the particular ranges of movement that are required. Doors that have to open both ways (for example, the doors from restaurants into their kitchens) need different kinds of hinges from ordinary doors that open one way only. A mammal that stands and walks with its feet under its body [PLATE 46] needs differently constructed hip and shoulder joints from a reptile or a platypus that keeps its feet well out to the side [PLATES 47 and 48].

In bones that have been cleaned thoroughly for museum display, the surfaces that articulate at the joints have a matte texture. Bones fresh from the butcher look quite different, for their joint surfaces are covered by a shiny layer of cartilage. That covering is an essential part of the lubrication system that makes our joints move smoothly.

The wheels of a neglected bicycle turn stiffly and squeak, but a little oil will make them rotate freely and smoothly. Not only are the shafts of an unlubricated vehicle hard to turn, but if the vehicle is used friction heats the bearings and they may suffer severe damage. It can be a very expensive mistake to continue driving your car after the oil warning light has come on. Similarly, human and animal joints in which surfaces slide over each other need lubrication. The lubricant is synovial fluid, a watery fluid made viscous by big molecules of a protein-sugar complex. The fluid is prevented from seeping entirely

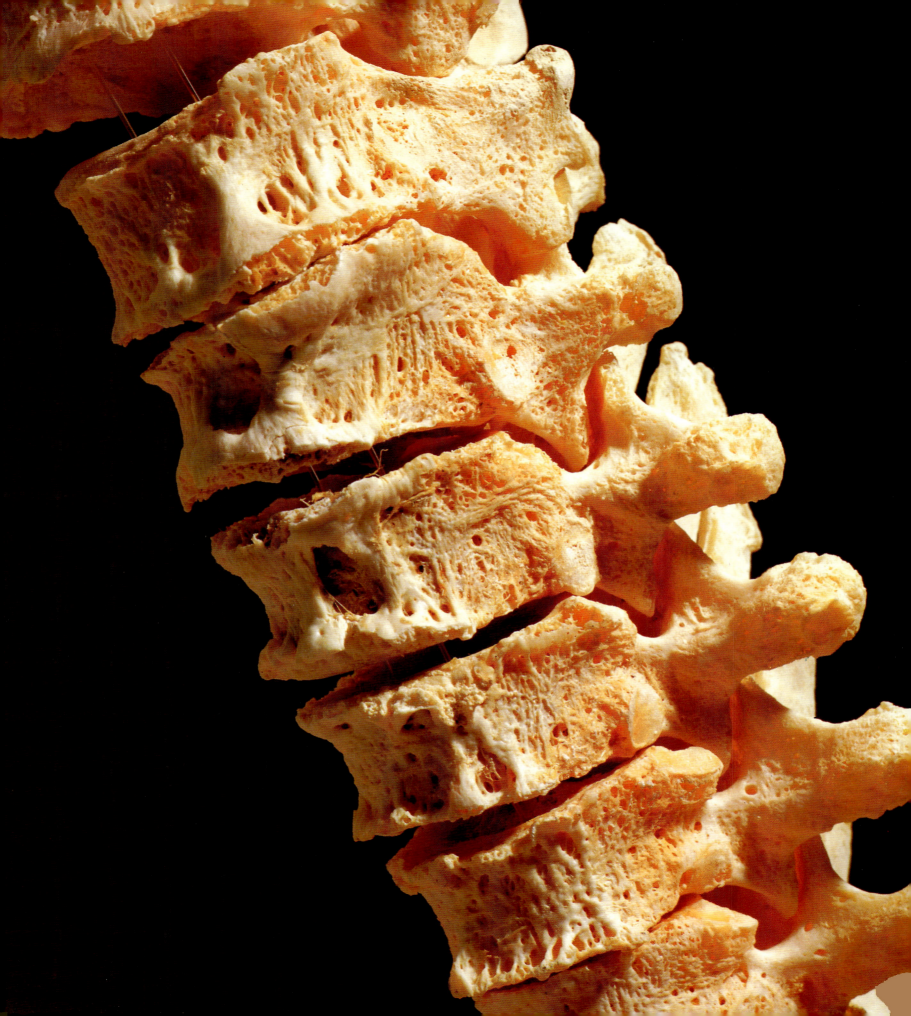

away by a bag (the joint capsule) which encloses the joint, but some means is needed of getting it between the articulating surfaces and keeping it there. In machines this is achieved in two main ways. In hydrostatic lubrication there is a small hole in each bearing through which oil is pumped, into the gap between axle and bearing, to replace the oil that gets squeezed out. In hydrodynamic lubrication a rotating shaft drags the viscous oil along with it, constantly bringing a new supply of oil under the shaft where it is needed. Neither of these mechanisms can keep animal joints satisfactorily lubricated because animals have no oil pumps and because their joints do not rotate constantly in one direction, like the shafts of a machine.

When animals run, large forces act on their leg joints while the foot is on the ground but not when the foot is off the ground. That gives an opportunity for synovial fluid to get back into the gaps where it is needed as a lubricant, but some means is needed of preventing it being squeezed out again too soon, when the forces become large again. The cartilage provides that means.

Cartilage consists of a network of collagen fibers in a jelly-like matrix. It is much less stiff than bone, so the cartilage that covers joints flattens under pressure, increasing the area of near-contact and so increasing the distances that the viscous lubricant would have to flow to be squeezed out of the narrow gap. The cartilage also is rather spongy, so it soaks up fluid whenever the forces are low. These two properties of cartilage make animal joints work much better than they would do if bone pressed directly on bone.

Cartilage is much weaker than compact bone. For that reason, the large loads on joints must be spread out over fairly large areas of cartilage, so large joint surfaces are needed. Large contact areas are in any case needed to make squeeze-out distances large. That is why long bones often have swollen ends. These are usually supported from within by a filling of spongy bone. This gives the required support over a wide area without being too heavy. Also, it provides a less rigid base than compact bone would do, cushioning the delicate cartilage against impacts. Damage may nevertheless occur: the disabling consequence is osteoarthritis [PLATE 49].

In this chapter we have seen how bones are jointed together, either by flexible connectors as in the spine or by joints in which surfaces slide over each other, requiring lubrication. Examples from limbs and jaws have shown us how joints with different structures allow different degrees of freedom of movement, and we have discussed the numbers of degrees of freedom that are needed in legs. In the next chapter we will discuss the muscles that move the joints.

PLATE 49

Osteoarthritic human backbone.
Homo sapiens
Osteoarthritis is often the result of damage by severe exercise, but also often occurs without obvious cause.

Chapter 4

MUSCLE ATTACHMENTS

———

PLATE 50

Skeleton of a flounder.
Paralichthys lethostigma
Bones at the bases of the fins provide
attachments for fin muscles.

IN this chapter, examples ranging from the jaws of a warthog to the legs of a mole will show us how muscles move the joints between bones, how muscles are arranged to perform their tasks as effectively as possible, and how the form and texture of bones often reveals the attachment points for the muscles that worked them in the living animal.

We will start by looking at some of those small bones at the bases of fish fins that can be tiresomely difficult to get rid of when you eat fish [PLATE 50]. Each fin is supported by a series of bony rays that can be raised to spread the fin like a fan, or lowered to fold it flat against the body. When the fin is spread the rays can be swung from side to side, and fish often swim slowly by side-to-side movements of the rays, each ray moving slightly out of synchrony with the next, so that waves of movement travel along the fin. There is a ball-and-socket joint between each ray and the bones (called pterygiophores) at its base. The muscles that move the rays lie alongside the pterygiophores, attached to them and to the bases of the rays. Each pterygiophore carries two muscles on each side, partly separated by a little ridge on the bone. When the two muscles at the front of the pterygiophore shorten they raise the ray, and when the two at the rear shorten they fold it down again. When the two muscles on the left shorten they swing the ray over to the left, and when the two on the right shorten they swing it to the right. For every muscle there is another

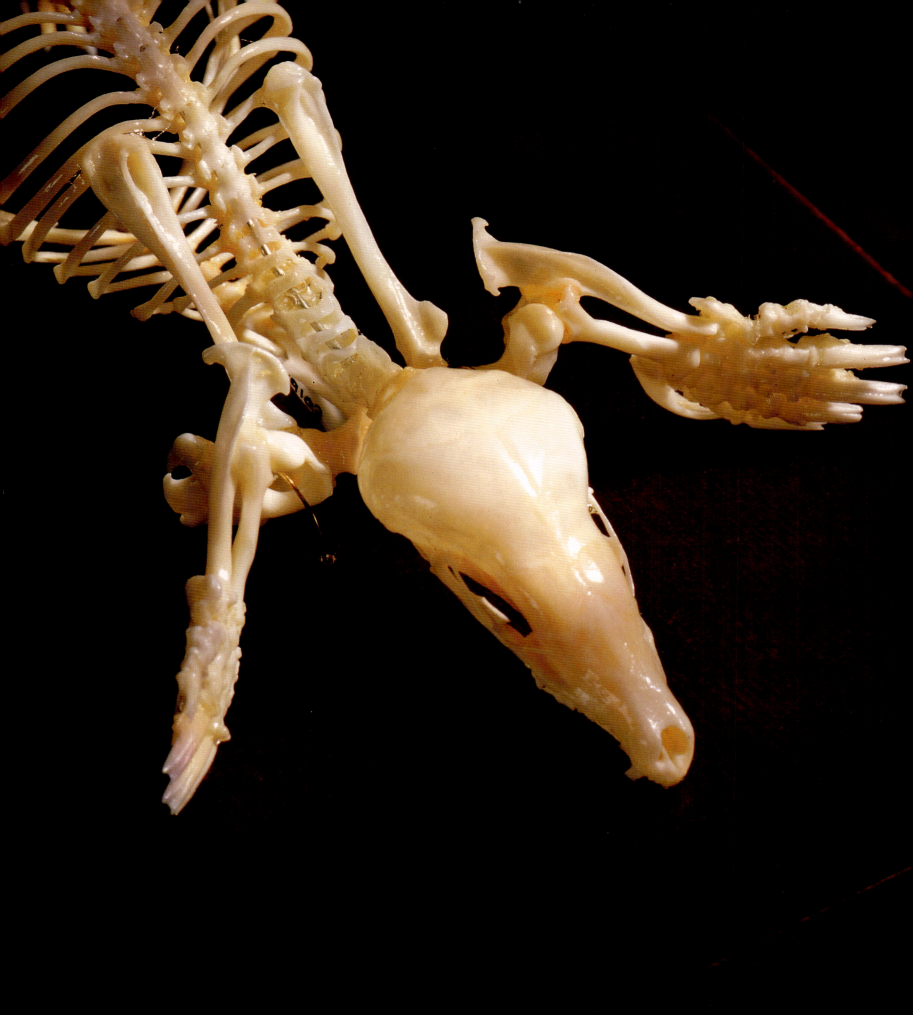

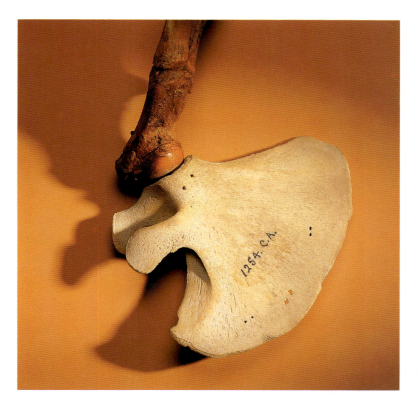

PLATE 52

Shoulder blade and humerus of a
Common Dolphin.
Delphinus delphis
The shoulder muscles are small, in
comparison with land mammals.

PLATE 51

Skeleton of a European Mole.
Talpa europaea
Strong muscles in the shoulder region
powered the digging forelegs.

PLATE 53

Sternum (breast bone) of a
Bald Eagle.
Haliaeetus leucocephalus
The wing muscles attach to
the deep keel.

that has the opposite effect: this is the principle of muscle antagonism.

The skeleton of a mole [PLATE 51] is shaped to accommodate huge forelimb muscles, used for digging the burrows that the mole patrols in search of its earthworm food. Most mammals have the shoulders beside the rib cage, leaving a slender neck between shoulders and head. The mole, however, has its shoulders farther forward, and instead of a neck there is a great mass of digging muscles between the ribs and the head. The largest muscle is the teres major, running from the (surprisingly slender) shoulder blade to a short, broad humerus (upper arm bone). Another important digging muscle is the triceps, which straightens the elbow. It attaches to the bony projection behind the elbow, popularly known as the funny bone, because knocking a nerve that runs over it gives humans an unpleasant tingling sensation. Moles have very large funny bones.

In moles, as in other mammals, the shoulder blade is not a flat plate but has a keel standing up from it. This separates muscles—not the big teres major, which attaches only to the rear end of the shoulder blade, but the smaller muscles that hold the head of the humerus in its socket, preventing shoulder dislocation. There is a muscle in front of the keel, one behind, and a third on the hidden face of the shoulder blade.

The forelimb of a dolphin is much less muscular than that of a mole, and this shows on its skeleton [PLATE 52]. It is a flipper used only for steering. (The main power for swimming comes from the tail.) It does not have to support the animal's weight, let alone dig, so can make do with relatively small muscles. The shoulder blade is relatively small and its very low keel shows that it was covered only by a thin layer of shoulder muscles. Notice how little room there is, especially for the muscle in front of the keel.

Another bone with a keel that separates two muscles is shown in PLATE 53. This is the sternum (breast bone) of a bird, the bone that is exposed when you carve the breast meat off a roast turkey. These muscles are the biggest in the body (a sixth or more of body mass, in most birds) and power the flapping of the wings in flight. You can judge how large they are from the photograph, because they fill the whole space between the sternum and the skin which wraps over the edge of the keel. Wing muscles, however, are useless for kiwis, which run on the ground and cannot fly. Their wings and wing muscles have become tiny vestiges in the course of evolution and the sternum is small, with no trace of a keel [PLATE 54].

You might think birds would need muscles on their backs to raise the wings, as well as muscles on their breasts to flap them down. In fact the downstroke is the main power stroke of flight, and the upstroke could be

PLATE 55

The skeleton of a Bald Eagle's trunk.
Haliaeetus leucocephalus
The skeleton is lying on its back.
The hole for the tendon of the
supracoracoideus muscle is visible
on the far side.

SUPRACORACOIDEUS
MUSCLE

HUMERUS

WISHBONE

PECTORALIS
MUSCLE

STERNUM

FIGURE D

A diagram showing how a bird's wing
muscles are attached to the skeleton.
The pectoralis muscle pulls the wing
down and the supracoracoideus
muscle raises it.

PLATE 54

Sternum (breast bone) and ribs of
Common Kiwi.
Apteryx australis
The wings and wing muscles are
rudimentary and the sternum has no keel.

passive if the bird simply allowed the aerodynamic forces on the wings to lift
them, but birds do have small wing-raising muscles, which assist the upstroke
and are also needed for spreading the wings for take-off. Surprisingly, these
muscles as well as the downstroke ones attach to the sternum. To raise the
wing, the muscle exploits the principle of the pulley. It connects to a tendon
that runs upward, through a hole in the shoulder girdle above the shoulder
joint, and then curls over to attach to the humerus [FIGURE D and PLATE 55].
The tendon works like a rope running over a pulley, but instead of a pulley
wheel there is simply a smooth, rounded surface on the bone, covered with
cartilage and lubricated like joints between bones.

The jaw muscles of a turtle [PLATE 56] also use the pulley principle. They
pull around a corner as they curve around the bone of the ear region to attach
to the big crest at the back of the skull. I want to use this example, however,
to illustrate another mechanical principle, the principle of levers. Alice
Sinclair, when a graduate student in my laboratory, set out to discover how
hard reptiles can bite. She constructed a bar with strain gauges built into it in
such a way that if the bar was bitten, the strain gauges registered the force.
It was not too hard to persuade the turtles to bite the bar; the hard part for
Alice was not getting bitten herself. She found that a 1 kilogram (2 pound)
freshwater turtle, a pet with a particularly vicious reputation, could bite with

PLATE 56

Skull of a Painted Turtle.
Chrysemys picta
The principal jaw muscles attached
to the crest at the rear of the skull.

the front of its mouth with forces up to at least 60 newtons (13 pounds force). This force acted 30 millimeters (12 inches) from the jaw joint but the muscles pulled on the jaw only 14 millimeters (5.5 inches) from the joint. The principle of levers tells us that the force exerted by the muscles must have been 60 x 30/14 = 130 newtons (29 pounds force).

Engineers describe the effectiveness of lever systems by calculating the mechanical advantage, the output force divided by the input force. In the case we are considering the output—the bite force—is 60 newtons and the input—the muscle force—is 130 newtons, so the mechanical advantage is 60/130 = .47. This may seem poor design, if there is an advantage in biting hard. Man-made devices for exerting large forces (for example, nutcrackers) have mechanical advantages much more than one: the output force is larger than the input force. In contrast, nearly all animal lever systems have mechanical advantages less than one, giving output forces less than the input force. Indeed, the turtle jaw's mechanical advantage of .47 is quite high by animal standards.

Alice found an even lower mechanical advantage for the jaw muscles of a caiman, a close relative of alligators [PLATE 57]. She found that a 1.3 kilogram (3 pound) caiman could bite with its front teeth with a maximum force of only 39 newtons (3 pounds force). This was 110 millimeters (44 inches) from the jaw joint, and the various muscles acted 30 millimeters (12 inches) or less

PLATE 57

Skull of an American Alligator.
Alligator mississippiensis
These jaws are designed for speed of
closing rather than strength.

PLATE 58

Knee joint of a young Rock Dassie.
Procavia capensis
The kneecap affects the leverage of
the muscle that attaches to it.
The separate epiphyses (end pieces) on
the bones show that this small hoofed,
rodent-like mammal was young.

from the joint, so the mechanical advantage was 30/110 = .27 or less and the muscles must have been exerting a total of at least 144 newtons (32 pounds force). Because the caiman has relatively longer jaws than the turtle, its muscles have to contract more strongly, to produce considerably less bite force. Of course, caimans, like people, can exert larger forces with their back teeth than with their front ones because they are nearer the jaw joint, giving a bigger mechanical advantage. Alice found that the caiman could exert 100 newtons (22 pounds force) when it bit with its back teeth.

Mechanical advantage affects speed of movement as well as force. The front of the turtle jaw exerts only about half as much force as the muscles, because it is about twice as far from the jaw joint. For the same reason, the front of the jaw moves twice as far as the muscles shorten, when the turtle closes its mouth. It moves twice as far in the same time, so it moves at double the speed of the shortening muscles. In contrast, the caiman's front teeth exert only .27 times the muscle force, but they close at 1/.27 = 3.7 times the muscle's rate of shortening. Thus the difference of mechanical advantage can be expected to give the turtle a slow, strong bite and the caiman a fast, weak one. Speed seems likely to be important to the caiman, which catches fish by grabbing them with its jaws. The turtle feeds on plants and slow-moving worms and snails, so it does not need a fast jaw action.

The difference between turtle and caiman jaw muscles is like the difference between gears on a bicycle. In low gear, each revolution of my bicycle's pedals turns the back wheel through one revolution and in high gear each turn of the pedals revolves the wheel four times. The low gear gives slow, forceful cycling (good for climbing hills), while the high gear is better for speed on the flat. The turtle has a forceful low-gear jaw and the caiman a fast high-gear one.

Leg muscles as well as jaw muscles work with different mechanical advantages in different animals. For example, the mole forelegs [PLATE 51] seem designed for digging strength, with relatively large mechanical advantages, and horse forelegs seem designed for running speed, with lower mechanical advantages. The olecranon process (funny bone) at the elbow is longer, in proportion to leg length, in moles than in horses, giving the triceps muscle which attaches to it a larger mechanical advantage. The mole is like a bicycle in low gear and the horse like one in high gear.

The kneecap is part of a mechanism that changes the mechanical advantage of the muscles that extend the knee. These muscles are in the front of the thigh, attached at their upper end mainly to the femur (thigh bone). At their lower end, they form a tendon which runs around the knee to attach to the tibia (shin bone). This is not ordinary tendon for its whole length. Where it rounds the knee, it is expanded and hardened to form a bony nodule, the kneecap [PLATE 58]. As the knee bends and extends, the kneecap slides up and down a groove in the end of the femur. Lubricated cartilage surfaces on the groove and on the kneecap ensure that it runs smoothly.

It used to be thought that the groove in the femur functioned as a simple pulley, like the bar of bone that the wing-raising tendon runs over in birds [FIGURE D]. Now we realize that the mechanism is more complicated. A pulley wheel is circular, centered on its axle, but the groove of the femur forms a spiral curve around the axis of the knee joint. Consequently, the force in the part of the tendon below the kneecap may be different from the force in the part above. The principle is that of lifting heavy loads by pushing them up gentle ramps, only the other way around. A gentle ramp enables a small force to raise a heavy weight, but the ramp-like slope of the spiral groove makes the force on the tibia less than the muscle force. This was demonstrated in an experiment in which force gauges were attached to the tendon above and below the knee cap on a human cadaver. The kneecap and spiral groove make knee movements weaker but faster.

We are going to think now about a force which, so far, we have ignored. The diagram of a typical primitive reptile jaw [FIGURE E, *left*] shows the bite force and the muscle force and also a third force, the reaction force of the jaw joint. The muscle force pulls the jaw firmly into its socket so the skull presses as shown on the jaw. The harder the reptile bites the bigger this force at the joint and the stronger the joint must be.

This mechanism made some changes to the jaw that occurred in the course of evolution seem very strange. Early reptiles had all their teeth in one large bone (the dentary) at the front of the lower jaw but there were several other

FIGURE E

The forces believed to have acted on the jaws of two extinct synapsid reptiles, when they bit with their back teeth. The jaw on the left is from a primitive synapsid reptile and the jaw on the right from an advanced one.

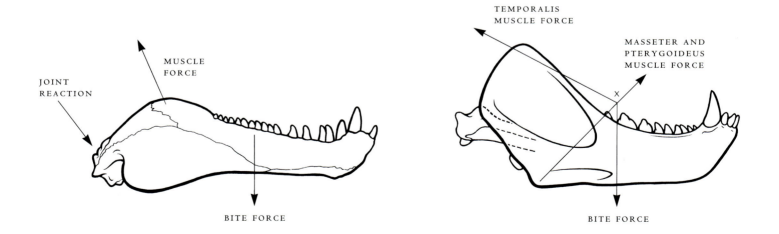

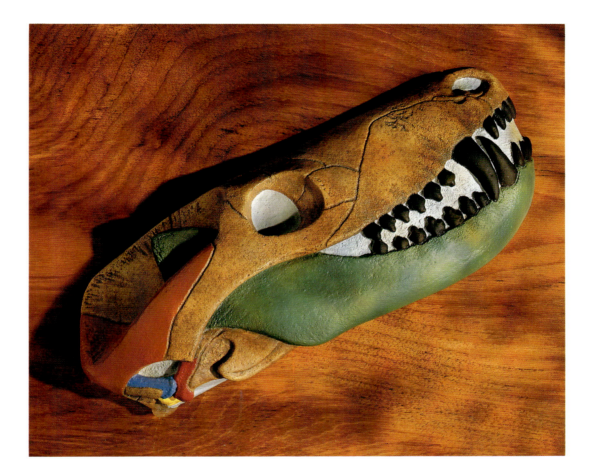

PLATE 59

Model of the skull of an
advanced synapsid reptile.
Thrinaxodon (Triassic period, about
220 million years ago)
As the mammals evolved from the
synapsid reptiles, the dentary bone
(green) became the sole bone of the
lower jaw, and the articular and
quadrate bones (red and blue,
respectively) became ear ossicles.

bones between it and the jaw joint, in the rear part of the jaw. The whole jaw was strongly built [FIGURE E, *left*].

The changes that I am going to describe occurred about 200 million years ago in the synapsid reptiles, the group from which the mammals (including ourselves) evolved. Fossils show us that the rear part of the dentary bone, where the jaw muscles must have attached, became greatly enlarged, indicating that the muscles were big and strong [PLATE 59]. Meanwhile, the bones of the rear part of the jaw, between the dentary and the jaw joint, became remarkably slender. Eventually some of them disappeared and others became mammalian ear bones, as explained in Chapter 7, while the dentary formed a new joint connecting it to the skull. The lower jaws of mammals consist of the dentary bone and nothing else.

The strange thing about this sequence of events is that the jaw joint became weaker as the jaw muscles apparently became stronger. In the transitional stage, when the rear jaw bones were slender and the new jaw joint was forming, the joint must have been very weak indeed. How could these reptiles have bitten hard, without breaking their jaws?

A possible solution to the problem was suggested by A.W. Crompton of Harvard University. Examination of the shape of the transitional skull and particularly of the areas on it where jaw muscles might have attached suggested that there were two main groups of jaw muscles, pulling in different directions. One muscle, the temporalis, apparently attached high up on the dentary bone and pulled upward and backward [FIGURE E, *right*]. Two others pulled upward and forward: a masseter muscle which attached low down on the outer side of the dentary, and a pterygoideus muscle on the inner side. The forward pull exerted by these two muscles would have been balanced by the backward pull of the temporalis, so the effect of both sets of muscles acting together would be equivalent to a single upward force acting through point X, where the lines of the muscle forces intersect. This could balance a downward force on the jaw due to food being bitten between the back teeth. In this case (if the upward and downward forces were equal and in line with each other) there would be no reaction force at the jaw joint, even when the back teeth were exerting a large force on the food. Strong jaw muscles do not necessarily imply the need for a strong jaw joint. These animals, however, would have had to be careful when biting with their front teeth, because the forces would not then be in line and (as in the turtle) there would have been a reaction force at the joint.

The re-formed jaw joint is strong again in mammals but the arrangement of jaw muscles pulling in different directions survives, as a tiger skull shows

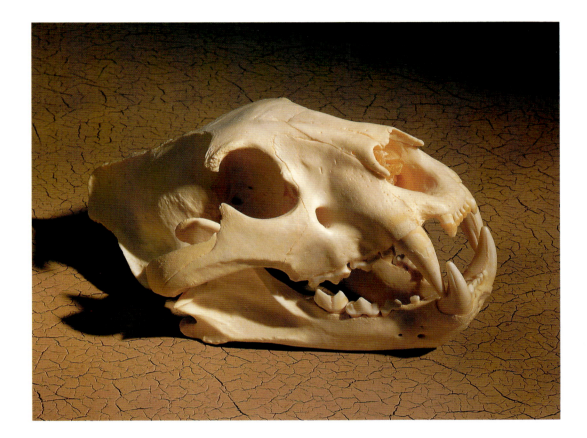

PLATE 60

Skull of a Tiger.
Panthera tigris
The large temporalis muscle filled the
space that is in shadow behind the eye
socket. The masseter muscle ran from
the lower edge of the lower jaw to the
zygomatic arch (cheek bone).

us [PLATE 60]. To understand where the tiger's jaw muscles were, we need to know the layout of its skull. The snout is at the front and the braincase at the rear. On either side of the skull, like a pair of C-shaped handles, are the strips of bone called the zygomatic arches. A notch at the front end of the arch and a corresponding hollow between snout and braincase show where the eyeball fitted in. The jaw joint is at the rear end of the zygomatic arch [PLATE 39] and the upward projection (coronoid process) of the lower jaw fits into the space between the zygomatic arch and the braincase. The temporalis muscle runs from the coronoid process to the roof of the braincase (which it covers) pulling upward and backward as in synapsids. The masseter is a strip of muscle between the outer lower edge of the jaw and the zygomatic arch, pulling upward and forward. The internal pterygoideus muscle, whose position inside the jaw is hidden in the photograph, also pulls upward and forward.

It is apparent from the spaces available for them that the temporalis and masseter muscles are both large. The pterygoideus is relatively small; a big muscle inside the jaw would narrow the throat, making it difficult for the tiger to swallow large chunks of flesh. The jaw muscles were dissected from a tiger carcass and weighed: the temporalis accounted for 48% of the total mass, the masseter 45% and the internal pterygoideus only 7%. We will soon see that some other mammals have relatively much smaller temporalis muscles.

Tigers grab their prey not only with their claws, but also with the dagger-like canine teeth at the front of the jaws. They also use their front teeth for tearing hunks of flesh from carcasses. If they used jaw muscles that pulled directly upward to maintain their grip when pulling hard with their teeth, they would be in danger of dislocating their jaws. The temporalis, however, pulling not only upward but also backward, acts in the right direction to prevent the jaw from being pulled forward out of its joint sockets.

Horses [PLATE 61] have different habits and very different jaws and muscles. They feed on grass which needs grinding to make it digestible, and are not in the habit of tearing flesh. There is very little space for temporalis muscles behind the eye, and the coronoid process on the lower jaw is correspondingly small. The lower jaw, however, is very deep, leaving room for a large masseter muscle on its outer side and also a large pterygoideus inside. Because the food comes in small pieces, it does not matter if big pterygoideus muscles make the gullet narrower than that of a tiger. I have no measurements of horse jaw muscle masses but in zebra the temporalis makes up only 11% of total jaw muscle mass. As a general rule, flesh-eating mammals like tigers have large temporalis muscles and plant-eating mammals like horses and warthogs [PLATE 62] have small ones.

PLATE 61

Skull of a horse.
Equus caballus
There is very little room for a temporalis muscle behind the eye but there was a huge masseter muscle between the lower jaw and the cheek bone.

PLATE 62

Skull of a Warthog.
Phacochoerus aethiopicus
Ridges on the lower jaw show where
the tendons of the big masseter
muscle attached.

Tigers need long muscle fibers in their jaw muscles to enable them to open their mouths widely—muscles cannot exert much force if stretched more than 50% beyond their resting lengths. Warthogs have no need to open their mouths so wide, and can make do with shorter muscle fibers. This has left its mark on the warthog jaw. The parallel ridges on the jaw, where the masseter attached, are the lines of attachment of sheets of tendon [PLATE 62]. Rather than having relatively long masseter muscle fibers running all the way from jaw to zygomatic arch, the warthog has a larger number of shorter fibers running obliquely between sheets of tendon. This arrangement, packing in more, shorter muscle fibers, increases the force that the muscles can exert at the expense of a reduced range of movement.

This chapter has concentrated on the ways in which bones are shaped to suit the attachments of the muscles that move them. We have seen attachment areas for large muscles, such as the keels on the mole shoulder blade and the bird sternum. We have seen relatively large mechanical advantages in turtle jaws and mole legs and smaller ones that increase speed at the expense of force in caiman jaws and horse legs. We have seen how jaw muscles running in different directions may have enabled a mammal-like reptile to bite strongly without damaging a weak jaw joint, and how the relative sizes of different jaw muscles suit the different feeding habits of tigers and horses. For a final example of how bones may be molded by the need for muscle attachments, look back at the sloth pelvis [PLATE 24] and see how it provides a rim for the attachment of the muscles of the abdominal wall. The corresponding attachment in humans gives a fat man's belly a well-defined lower edge.

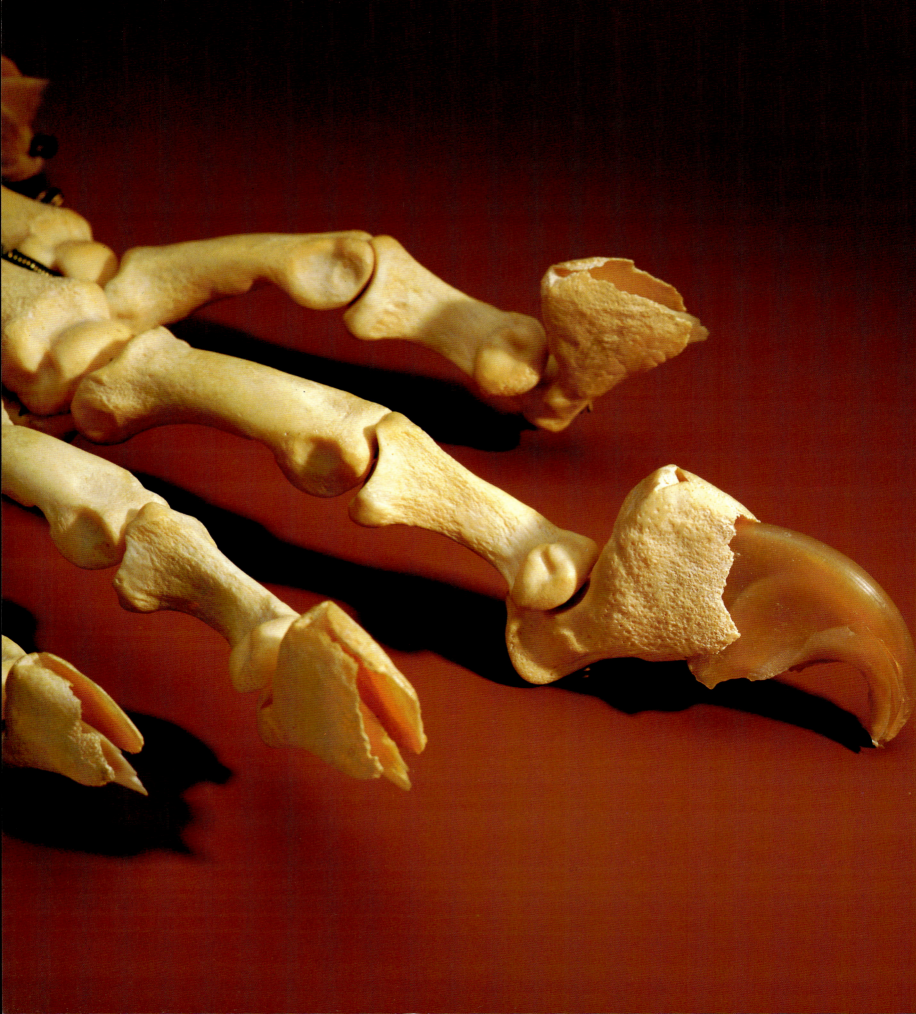

Chapter 5

MECHANISMS

———

IN Chapter 4 we saw how the movements of bones and the forces that act on them are controlled by muscles in (generally) fairly obvious ways. This chapter is about some less obvious skeletal mechanisms. First we will examine two cases in which springs as well as muscles are concerned in moving bones. After that we will look at the unexpected way in which fishes open their mouths. Next we will find out that a parrot's skull belongs to a class of mechanisms well known to engineers, and finally we will see how subtle and complicated animal mechanisms can be, and yet work well.

Our two examples of springs are both ligaments. Ligaments connect bones to each other whereas tendons, as we have seen, connect muscles to bones. For example, the cruciate ligaments of the knee, which are often broken in sports accidents, connect the femur (thigh bone) to the tibia (shin bone). Tendons and most ligaments, including the cruciate ligaments, are formed from collagen fibers that are strong and can stretch only a little. The ligaments in our two examples, which function as springs, are formed from elastin, a much more rubber-like protein. It can be stretched to about double its initial length, and recoils immediately and completely
when released.

The ligamentum nuchae is a stout band of elastin running along the back of the neck, close under the skin in camels, cattle, antelopes, horses and other

PLATE 63

Skeleton of a Lion's paw.
Panthera leo
Elastic ligaments make the claws spring back into their sheaths when they are not being used.

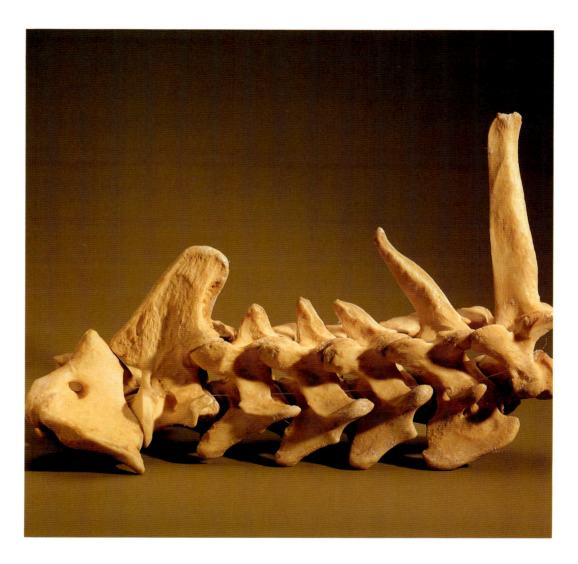

PLATE 64

Neck vertebrae of a Brazilian Tapir.
Tapirus terrestris
The elastic neck ligament attached to
the spines that stand up from the
vertebrae.

hoofed mammals. It runs from the back of the skull to the lower back, attaching on the way to the tall spines of the vertebrae [PLATES 46 and 64]. It serves as a guy rope, helping to hold the animal's head high, but can stretch enough for the animal to lower its head to the ground to feed. It is always under tension in intact animals, so when the ligament in a carcass is cut the cut ends spring apart. In experiments with roe deer carcasses my colleagues and I found that in the animal's alert position, with head raised, the ligament was stretched to 1.4 times its slack length; and that when the head was lowered to eat from the ground it was 1.7 times its slack length. The carcasses of dead sheep and deer often have the neck pulled back to an unnatural angle by the elastic tension of this ligament.

Our measurements on deer indicated that the head was well supported by the ligament in the feeding position, but less completely supported by it in the alert position. On the other hand, we found in a simple experiment with a camel carcass in Nairobi that if we pulled the neck horizontal (with the dead animal resting on its belly on the floor) it sprang back up to the alert position when released. Deer may have to use muscles to help support the head, and camels may have to use muscles to pull the head down for feeding.

The ligamentum nuchae of a large mammal is an impressive structure. When I wanted to measure the extensibility of the camel's, I could not find weights heavy enough to stretch this ligament much, and performed the experiment by tying one end to a beam and asking two carefully-weighed technicians to swing from the other. Even it, however, was small compared to the ligamentum nuchae of a giraffe I dissected in the field, working rather nervously because we were uncertain whether the lions who had killed it were still hiding in the nearby thicket. The ligament was about 2.5 meters (8 feet) long and its cross-sectional area was no less than 50 square centimeters (8 square inches).

The elastin springs of my second example are very much smaller. Cats (including lions and tigers) protrude their claws when they are required for use, but when the toe muscles relax the claws spring back into their sheaths [PLATE 63]. This happens because the bone at the tip of each toe, which bears the claw, is connected to the next bone in the toe by an elastin ligament. When the claw is protruded the ligament is stretched, and when the muscles relax the ligament's elastic recoil pulls the claw back in.

These mechanisms need springs to function, but most others depend entirely on muscles without the assistance of springs. Some muscles, such as those in the heads of fish, act in remarkably indirect ways. Fish skulls are extraordinarily complicated, with over 100 bones, for example, in the head of

There are muscles between the braincase and the suspensorium that swing the suspensoria out sideways to enlarge the mouth cavity and inwards again to narrow it, to pump water over the gills for breathing. The electrical recordings also show that a large muscle in the throat, inactive in normal breathing, has a major role in sucking food into the mouth.

To understand how this throat muscle works we have to think of the skull as a three-dimensional mechanism. In the underside of the fish's head between the lower jaws are the ceratohyal bones, arranged to form a V [FIGURE F, *right*]. The muscle we are discussing connects the point of the V to the shoulder girdle behind the head. When it shortens it pulls the point of the V towards the rear, making the arms of the V splay apart, pushing on the suspensorium and so widening the mouth cavity. Thus a muscle in the mid-line of the throat enlarges the mouth cavity to suck food in.

We will return to fish later to discuss an even more complicated mechanism, but before that we will look at some simpler mechanisms in other animals.

The wings of birds carry two groups of large feathers: the primary feathers which are supported by the bones of the modified hand and the secondary feathers which are supported by the forearm.

As in humans the bird forearm has two parallel bones, the radius and ulna [PLATE 66]. However, their attachments to humerus (the upper arm bone) and hand are different from those of the corresponding bones in our arms. The arrangement in birds links the movements of elbow and wrist so that when one bends the other must bend too, and when one extends the other extends [FIGURE G, *right*]. When the wing is folded, both joints are bent, and when it is extended for flight, both are extended.

There are four elements in this mechanism: the two parallel bones (radius and ulna), the wrist bones that connect their outer ends together and the humerus at their inner ends. This is an example of a four-bar mechanism, a class of mechanism considered fundamental by engineers. Take three rigid bars and attach them together with hinge joints, forming a triangle, and you will have a rigid structure. Hinge four bars together as a quadrilateral, however, and you have a moveable mechanism. Hold one bar stationary and move one of the others, and the remaining two will move in a precisely predictable way: the mechanism has one degree of freedom of movement. Add one more bar to make five, however, and the predictability is lost. A five-bar loop has two degrees of freedom of movement. Thus four-bar loops are special, the ultimate simple mechanism. (I have assumed that the axes of the hinge joints are parallel to each other. A four-bar loop with non-parallel hinge joints is rigid.)

PLATE 66

Fossil of an *Archaeopteryx lithographica.* (Jurassic period, about 150 million years ago)
As in modern birds (and ourselves) there are two bones in each forearm.

PLATE 69

Southern Pacific Rattlesnake skull.
Crotalus viridis
The mouth is open and the fangs
erect, ready for the strike.

PLATE 70

Southern Pacific Rattlesnake skull.
Crotalus viridis
The mouth is closed with the fangs
folded down.

PLATE 68

Skull of a Reticulated Python.
Python reticulatus
The many separately-moveable bones
enable the snake to swallow huge prey.

Chapter 6

TEETH

TEETH consist mainly of dentine (ivory), a material so much like bone that it seems reasonable to include a chapter about teeth in a book about bones. The smooth shiny surfaces of teeth contrast with the matte texture of the bones of a skull [PLATE 73] but that is because teeth are coated by an outer layer of enamel, a much harder substance that contains more calcium phosphate and less collagen.

This chapter describes many different kinds of teeth: long teeth and short ones, sharp teeth and blunt ones, massive tusks and teeth as slender and flexible as the bristles of a toothbrush. We will see how these many different kinds of teeth are used for catching prey, for cutting it up or crushing it and for various other purposes. We will look first at contrasting kinds of teeth used by fishes with different feeding habits, and then at the equally impressive variety of teeth possessed by mammals.

Mammals like us chew food before swallowing it, and much of the interest in mammal teeth is in seeing how they have been designed by evolution for breaking food up. Most fish, however, swallow their prey whole, and the main function of the teeth is for seizing it.

Predatory fishes capture their prey in two main ways, by snapping or by sucking. Snapping is much less common but we will look first at a fish that feeds that way. Our example [PLATE 72] is the gar pike, a primitive bony fish

PLATE 72

Lower jaw of Alligator Gar.
Lepisosteus spatula
The pointed teeth are good for grabbing prey.

PLATE 75

Skull of an Angler fish.
Lophius piscatorius
The long teeth fold down to admit
prey, and spring up to prevent it
escaping.

found in lakes and river backwaters in North America. It feeds on smaller fishes, dashing out to catch them from its ambush among reeds. It gets its jaws alongside the intended victim, then grabs it with a sudden sideways flick of the head. The prey may be slippery, but the spikiness of the gar pike's teeth gives it a firm grip. This method of feeding catches the prey sideways-on in the mouth, which leaves the gar pike with a tricky problem: how can the prey be swallowed? The predator may have to release its grip and grab the prey again several times, in the process of working it around to a position in which it is facing down the gar's throat. Prey fish go down the gullet most easily if they are swallowed head first.

That seems an awkward and risky way to swallow: if the prey is not yet dead, releasing the grip to turn it around may give it an opportunity to escape. Perch, which are also predators, set about swallowing in a quite different way, sucking prey into the mouth with a sudden huge expansion of the head. Some jockeying for position may be needed so that the unfortunate prey is facing the predator, but once that has been achieved the rest is accomplished neatly: the perch opens its mouth and sucks, and the prey is drawn in. Obviously, the prey will try to swim away to safety, but the faster the predator sucks the less likely is it to be able to get away. I know no measurements of the sucking speed for perch, but high-speed films have been taken of trout feeding in water with tiny polystyrene spheres suspended in it. The spheres had the same density as the water so they moved with it and their speed, measured from the film, was the speed of the water. The measurements showed water entering the trout's mouth at over 1 meter (39 inches) per second, a lethal speed for any small prey fish unable to swim so fast.

The speed at which the water enters the mouth cavity is the rate of enlargement of the cavity, divided by the area of the mouth opening. Other things being equal, the smaller the mouth opening the faster the water, carrying the prey with it, will flow into the mouth cavity. If the perch had big teeth like *Hydrolycus* [PLATE 74], perhaps it would have to open its jaws wider to let the food in, so it could not suck so fast. Instead, the teeth are tiny, so small that you have to look carefully to see them individually. They cover the surfaces of the upper and lower jaws making them rough like sandpaper, giving this predator a good friction grip on its prey. If the prey is not drawn right into the mouth with the first suck, the perch should be able to keep a firm grip on it while preparing to suck again.

The Angler fish [PLATE 75] is a suction feeder with big teeth, but some of its teeth are very special and must count among the most vicious products of evolution. They are long, curved, very sharp and (this is the vicious bit)

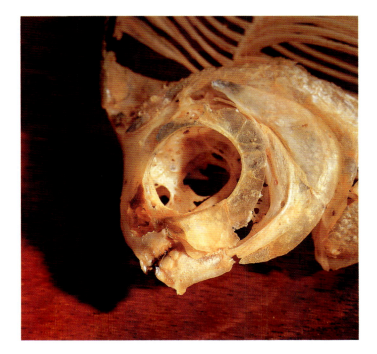

PLATE 77

Myleus rubripinnis
This fish and its close relative the pacu have chisel-like teeth, good for taking bites from leaves and fruit.

Many years ago at the start of my scientific career I was a member of an expedition to Guyana. We set up camp in the rain forest on the bank of a stream, where I researched piranha and other fish while my colleagues studied insects. The whole expedition turned out to help with my fishing on the understanding that, if I had the front half of each fish for study, the rest could be curried for dinner. We had trouble with piranha escaping by biting through the fishing line until we took to attaching the hooks to quite thick wire, and even then the fish occasionally got away by biting through the hook.

The pacu is a much larger relative of the piranha, living in the same area but feeding on water plants and on fruits that fall into the water from over-hanging trees. It was a regular food of the indigenous Indians, who used to shoot it with bows and arrows as it swam by: a cord attached to the arrow enabled them to pull the prey in. Like its notorious relative, the pacu has cutting teeth, but they would be little use for cutting flesh. Instead of being knife-like blades as in the piranha, they are much broader, more like chisels. I caught a related species, *Myleus*, with similar teeth [PLATE 77] and found its stomach filled with fragments of leaves, each fragment with neatly scalloped edges which exactly fitted the scalloped line of teeth.

Sharks cut pieces from large prey, as piranhas do, but their jaws work like saws rather than shears. The teeth of the saw are the triangular teeth with sharp serrated edges, in the shark's upper jaw [PLATE 78]: the lower teeth are

PLATE 78

Jaws of a Great White Shark.
Carcharodon carcharias
The triangular teeth saw
through flesh.

PLATE 82

A view down the throat of an
American Alligator skull.
Alligator mississippiensis
The internal openings of the nasal
passages are in sharp focus at the
center of the picture.

PLATE 81

Pharyngeal teeth of a drum fish.
Pogonias fasciatus
These teeth in the throat are used
for crushing mollusks.

simply spikes that grip the prey. The shark grabs its victim and then threshes around, shaking its head violently. If the movements of the prey kept pace with the shark's head, the teeth would remain stationary in it and there would be no saw action. In practice, the inertia of the prey makes it lag behind, so that the shark's teeth move relative to it and saw into the prey. The process is rather slow and very messy, but it is effective. Large sharks such as the Great White Shark, which grows to a length of 7 meters (23 feet), can bite the limbs off human adults. However, one leg found in a shark's stomach had been cut off neatly with a knife—and that led to a murder enquiry.

Most of the well-known kinds of fishes (trout, perch, cod, flounders and many others) belong to the group known as the teleosts, which have skeletons made of bone. Some other kinds of fishes also have bony skeletons but are not included in the teleosts: for example the gar pike has thick scales and other primitive features that show that it belonged to the holosteans, a group that flourished at the time of the dinosaurs and included ancestors of the teleosts. Sharks, however, are cartilaginous fishes, members of a group that is only very remotely related to the teleosts. Their skeletons are built of cartilage rather than of bone. The bony appearance of the shark's jaws [PLATE 78] is due to the cartilage being impregnated with calcium phosphate, making it white and fairly hard, and the only truly bone-like tissues in the skeleton are the dentine of the teeth and scales, and some bone at the scale bases. The rays are also cartilaginous fishes, but their teeth do not form saws. Eagle rays [PLATE 79] feed on mollusks and crustaceans and have pavements of flat teeth to crush them. Sharp teeth would be blunted and probably chipped by mollusk shells, but these flat teeth do the job well.

We return to the teleosts with their bony skeletons for the rest of our examples of fish teeth. We will turn from the crushing teeth of eagle rays to the opposite extreme of tooth structure. The catfishes are (mostly) freshwater fishes with whisker-like barbels that serve as feelers and suggest the whiskers of a cat. The group has many bizarre members, the oddest being the loricariid catfishes of South America. These have their bodies enclosed in an armor of plates of bone. The mouth is on the underside of the head and is surrounded by lips that are expanded to form a sucker, rather like the rubber suckers that are fitted to toy arrows to prevent children from blinding each other. These catfishes live in streams, holding onto rocks with their suckers—that way they escape the effort of having to swim to avoid being washed downstream. Their teeth are long, slender and flexible, just like the bristles of a toothbrush [PLATE 80]. While the fish is holding onto the rock by suction, it is also brushing off the green algae that grow on submerged surfaces of rocks with its teeth. These algae are its food. Loricariid catfishes are often kept in tropical aquariums and do a useful job, cleaning the algae off the glass. If one is feeding on the near side of the tank you can look through the glass into its mouth and see the teeth working away.

Fish may use their teeth for grabbing, cutting, crushing and even (as we have just seen) brushing, but few actually chew, making repeated jaw movements to break food up. Among those few, the most plentiful are the members of the carp family which (paradoxically) have no teeth in their jaws. The teeth that they chew with are well back in the throat, mounted on the greatly enlarged skeleton of the last pair of gills. These jaws are in the floor of the throat and are pulled up by large muscles which press the teeth against a horny pad on the underside of the skull. The food is squeezed and torn between the teeth and the horny pad.

Some other fishes use teeth in the throat for crushing mollusks. The impressive teeth of the drum fish [PLATE 81], which is not a member of the carp family, are in the upper as well as lower part of its throat.

There is a good reason for such fishes to have their crushing and chewing teeth in their throats. Fish breathe in through their mouths, and if the mouth were blocked by a mass of food they would have to stop breathing while they chewed. With their teeth behind the gills, carp have no difficulty in breathing while chewing.

A similar problem is overcome by crocodiles in a different way. They feed largely on water birds, or mammals that come to the water to drink. They grab this prey with a snap of the jaws, then hold it under water to drown. That is quite an effective method of killing but it would be a pity (from the crocodile's point of view) if the crocodile drowned first. Not only is its mouth blocked by the prey, but it must keep its mouth underwater if the prey is to drown. How then can the crocodile breathe? Its nostrils are at the tip of its snout but do not connect through into the front part of the mouth cavity, as the nostrils of lizards do. Instead there is a bone-enclosed passageway in the palate, leading all the way back to a pair of openings at the back of the mouth [PLATE 82]. These make a direct connection with the windpipe, when the crocodile is not actually swallowing, enabling it to breathe with its mouth under water. Mammals (including ourselves) have a similar but less impressive arrangement that enables us to breathe through our noses while our mouths are full. Its benefits become apparent when we have a running cold that blocks the nasal passage and leaves us gasping for breath as we chew.

We have already noticed the recurved teeth that give pythons such a firm grip on their prey [PLATE 68] and the deadly hypodermic-needle teeth of

molars that emphasize one or more of the functions of the multipurpose primitive teeth. In baboons and other monkeys, and also in humans, the molars have become square with blunt cusps. The piercing and shearing functions of the back teeth have been lost, leaving only crushing and grinding—suitable treatment for the typical monkey diet of (mainly) leaves and fruit. In contrast, cats and hyenas have no crushing surfaces on their teeth. The only large teeth in the rear parts of their jaws are the blade-like carnassials. These have evolved from the primitive type of tooth by loss of the lower crushing heel and modification of the triangles into blades. The sharp carnassials of cats are good for slicing flesh but the more heavily built carnassials of hyenas are also used for cracking open bones [PLATE 86]. If cat carnassials are like pruning shears, hyena carnassials are like wire cutters. Dogs are less exclusively flesh-eating than cats and retain both cutting and crushing functions in their back teeth. They are using their carnassial teeth when they gnaw at a bone with the side of the mouth, scraping off the last of the flesh.

Monkeys, cats and hyenas have simpler teeth than their early mammal ancestors but still retain several cusps on each molar tooth. Dolphins also evolved from ancestors with fancy tooth patterns but their teeth are the simplest imaginable kind, each a simple spike [PLATE 87]. Evolution seems to have traveled from the simple teeth of most fishes and many reptiles, through the complicated type and back to the simple. Dolphin teeth are at least superficially like the teeth of gar pike [PLATE 72] and excellent for seizing hold of live prey. Dolphins feed mainly on fish and squid.

The rest of this chapter is about plant-eating mammals—horses, cattle, deer, rabbits and suchlike. Plant food consists of digestible foodstuffs in indigestible packaging. The contents of plant cells are sugars, starch, proteins, oils and other easily digested materials. The cell walls that enclose them consist largely of cellulose and other fibrous polymers that are much harder to digest. These can be broken down only slowly, and only with the help of microbes that live symbiotically in parts of the guts of plant-eating mammals (for example, the huge stomachs of cattle). Cereal grains, soft fruit and some other plant foods consist mainly of the digestible materials. Most of their food value can be obtained if they are crushed just enough to break open the cell walls. At the opposite extreme, mature leaves both of grasses and of broad-leaved plants consist mainly of fiber, with little that is easy to digest. Most of their food value is in the cell walls and they need thorough grinding. That breaks them up into small pieces, exposing more surface so the microbes can attack them faster. Cattle chew for around eight hours each day. All that chewing grinds the food thoroughly, but it also wears down the teeth.

PLATE 86

Skull of a Spotted Hyena.
Crocuta crocuta
The carnassial teeth at the rear of the jaws are formidable bone crackers, and are also useful for scraping flesh from bones.

which contains less protein and more calcium phosphate, so is harder and more brittle.

Not much is actually known about the properties of tooth materials, probably because it is difficult to find specimens large enough for testing in the machines that engineers use for testing metals and plastics. John Currey, the York University professor whose tests on bone have already been described, has also tested samples from tusks, which are exceptionally large teeth; but since tusks are not used for chewing the properties of their materials may not be typical. As well as elephant ivory, he tested samples from the tusk of a narwhal, a long, straight tusk used by males of this whale species for sparring [PLATE 88]. Both elephant dentine and narwhal dentine proved to be more flexible than ordinary bone, more like antler. This seems appropriate because tusks, like antlers, have to take knocks.

For teeth that are actually used for chewing, wear resistance is more important than impact strength—but the wear resistance of tooth materials has not been properly investigated. The only data I can quote come from a simple experiment by a group of my students who fixed a tooth from a dead sheep in a vice and bored into it with a dental drill. A weighted lever system made the drill press on the tooth with constant force. The students started the drill and observed the rate at which the drill sank into the tooth: it penetrated the enamel on the outside of the tooth very slowly, but when it reached the dentine it moved much faster. This showed that enamel is much more resistant to drilling than dentine, and suggests that it is also much more resistant to wear. If it is, the wear-resistant material is on the outside of the tooth, as seems sensible.

The enamel on human molar teeth is thick enough (up to 2.5 millimeters or .1 inch) not to wear through, at least on the diets generally eaten in developed countries. The enamel on the crowns of horse and cattle molars gets worn right through. Surprisingly, this has been turned to advantage in the course of evolution.

When horse and cattle teeth first emerge through the gums they have high cusps with bone-like material called cement between them [FIGURE 1 (2)]. These soon wear down [1 (3)] making the crown of the tooth relatively flat, but it is not polished smooth. The reason is that the dentine and cement, being less resistant to abrasion than the enamel, initially wear down faster, so the enamel comes to stand up in ridges above the surfaces of the dentine and cement [FIGURE 1 (3)]. Once that has happened, the enamel ridges give the other materials some protection, and all three materials continue to wear at equal rates, the enamel always standing a little proud of the worn surface: the

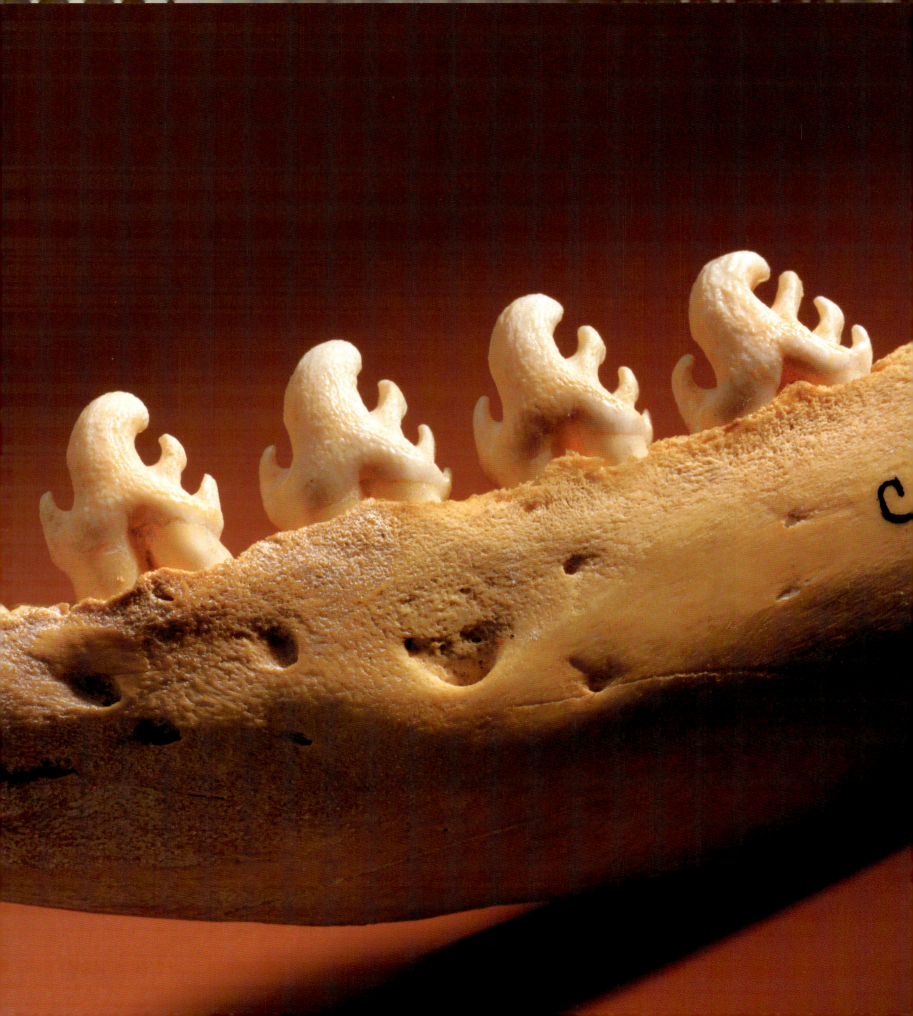

surface wears down but remains ridged like a file. Unlike our teeth, the molars of horses, cattle, buffaloes and capybaras continue to grow from the root throughout the animals' lives, so do not wear away. The principal ridges in cows and buffaloes run lengthwise along the jaw [PLATE 89] and the animal gets maximum advantage from them by chewing with a side-to-side motion. In contrast, grass-eating rodents such as the Capybara [PLATE 41] have enamel ridges running transversely across the teeth (making a wonderful file) and chew with a forward-and-back action.

These grinding teeth are self-sharpening files but the incisor teeth of rodents, such as the porcupine, are self-sharpening chisels [PLATE 90]. There is a pair each of these incisors in the upper and lower jaws. Squirrels use them to gnaw through the shells of nuts, to get at the kernels; the voles in our garden (where we have cherry trees) use them to gnaw into cherry stones; and beavers use them to gnaw the trunks of the trees that they fell to build their dams. Beavers are especially impressive gnawers: a pair working in shifts felled a 25-centimeter (10-inches) thick aspen tree in only four hours.

Rodents have a thick layer of enamel on the outer face of each incisor (it is orange in the porcupine but not on the inner face, so the outer edge of each tooth is the more resistant to wear and the teeth become chisel shaped. Notice the gap [PLATE 90] between the incisors and the grinding teeth. (Rodents have no canines.) A beaver can draw its lips across the gap so that they meet behind the incisors, closing off the rear part of the mouth. That enables the beaver to gnaw through a tree trunk without getting a mouthful of sawdust.

Like the grinding teeth of horses, cattle and some rodents, the gnawing incisors of rodents continue growing throughout their life, growing just fast enough to replace the material that wears away.

This chapter has introduced many different kinds of teeth. We have seen pointed, gripping teeth in gar pike, crocodiles and dolphins; cutting teeth in piranhas, sharks and lions; crushing teeth in rays and baboons; self-sharpening grinders in buffaloes and capybaras; gnawing teeth in rodents; and even some catfish teeth that resemble the bristles of toothbrushes. To finish the chapter, look at the fantastically shaped teeth of the Crab-eating Seal [PLATE 91]. Despite its name it does not eat crabs but krill, the shrimp-like animals that are also the principal food of the baleen whales. They take a mouthful from a shoal of krill, then strain out the water through the notches in their teeth. That way they avoid having to swallow too much water with their food.

Chapter 7

ACOUSTIC BONES

THIS chapter looks at bones in the light of the science of acoustics, considering some bones that help animals to hear and others that enable them to produce sounds. We will learn about tiny bones that carry into our ears sounds that would otherwise bounce off the sides of our heads. We examine how kangaroo rats manage to be exceptionally sensitive to faint sounds and how howler monkeys and cranes (the birds, not the machines) manage to be so noisy. We even consider the sounds that dinosaurs may have made. We will look first at hearing, and then at sound production.

Sound consists of tiny vibrations traveling through air or (for fish) through water. They really are tiny. When I speak to you across the table, neither whispering nor shouting, the vibrations of the air molecules that you detect have an amplitude of only about one ten thousandth of a millimeter. Amazingly, you not only detect my voice but can analyze the vibrations in sufficient detail to understand what I say. The tiny vibrations are accompanied by tiny pressure fluctuations. To get a very crude impression of what sound is like, think of a set of billiard balls set in a long, straight line, each a few millimeters from the next. If you gently tap the ball at one end it will move and hit the second ball, which will hit the third, and so on: a wave of collisions will travel along the line of balls. In that analogy, the balls represent air molecules. As sound travels through air, no molecule moves far, but the wave may

PLATE 92

Otolith of a Cod.
Gadus morhua
It looks like, but is not, bone.

be propagated to a very large distance. The pressure is greater where the molecules are close together than where they are far apart, so the vibrations are accompanied by pressure fluctuations.

For most fishes, hearing is straightforward. To sound waves, fish flesh seems much like water. The sound carries on as if the fish were not there so its whole body vibrates. The vibrations are detected by otolith organs, which are little cavities in the skull, each containing an otolith [PLATE 92], a stone-like lump of calcium carbonate and protein. The otoliths are denser than the fluid around them, so their inertia makes them move in their cavities as the fish is shaken by sound. These movements are detected by sense cells in the flexible connections between the otoliths and the cavity walls.

Our otolith organs are part of our inner ears but are not concerned with hearing. They make us aware of acceleration in a vehicle or a moving elevator, and tell us when our heads are tilted. It is another part of our inner ear—a small snail-like spiral (and not the conspicuous flap on the side of the head)—which is our sound detector.

For us and other land-living animals, hearing is much less simple than for fishes. The problem is that the sounds we want to hear are traveling in air, but our inner ears are filled with watery fluid. It is remarkably difficult to get sound to travel from air to water (or, for that matter, from water to air). When a sound wave traveling through air hits a water surface, only .1% of its energy gets through into the water: the rest is reflected back into the air. This is because air and water have very different properties. Not only is water about 700 times denser than air, but it is also much less compressible: a doubling of pressure from 1 atmosphere to 2 halves the volume of air but reduces the volume of water by less than one part in ten thousand.

To get an impression of the difficulty of transmitting sound from air to water, think of a line of balls of which the first few are table tennis balls (representing air) and the rest billiard balls (representing water). If the first table tennis ball is tapped it moves and collides with the second, making it hit the third—a wave of collisions is transmitted from ball to ball. However, when the last table tennis ball hits the first billiard ball, the heavy billiard ball hardly moves and the light table tennis ball bounces back, starting a wave traveling backward along the line of table tennis balls. Similarly, when sound traveling in air (a light compressible medium) hits the surface of water (heavy and incompressible) most of the sound energy is reflected and very little enters the water.

This problem is largely overcome, in amphibians and reptiles, by a very simple device. The sound arriving in the air hits an eardrum, a thin membrane

PLATE 93

Skull of a Spiny Softshell Turtle.
Trionyx ferox
The eardrum was stretched across
the round hollow that is in shadow,
above the rear end of the lower jaw.

PLATE 96

Model of human ear ossicles.
Homo sapiens
The actual stapes (the stirrup-shaped
ossicle) would be about 4 millimeters
(.2 inch) long.

which has air on both sides of it, so is easily made to vibrate. Its vibrations are then transmitted by a thin rod of bone (the stapes) to a small opening (the oval window) in the wall of the fluid-filled inner ear. The forces exerted by sound waves on the eardrum's relatively large area are transmitted by the stapes to the much smaller area of the oval window. Thus the pressure changes (force *per unit area*) are increased: the small pressure changes in the air set up much larger pressure changes in the ear. This overcomes the problem of transmitting sound from air to water.

The eardrum of a turtle is stretched across the round opening at the back of the skull [PLATE 93]. The cavity that you can see within this opening is the air-filled middle ear, across which sound is transmitted by the stapes to the oval window on its inner side.

The turtle eardrum is supported by a complete frame of bone but the frog eardrum has bone only down its front edge, where it fits into a notch in the skull. The stapes (an extremely thin rod) [PLATE 94] reach out to it from the oval window. The vibrations which frog eardrums make in response to sound have been measured by a technique involving laser light. It was found that the eardrum vibrates almost as much as open air would do if exposed to the same sound. This implies that the eardrum/stapes system is very effective, transmitting a large proportion of the sound energy that hits it into the inner ear, and reflecting only a little.

Lizards have big eardrums at the backs of their heads, just like frogs, but you will find no eardrums in snakes although they evolved from lizards. In snakes, the stapes remain [PLATE 95], but instead of connecting the oval window to the absent eardrum, it attaches to the quadrate, the bone that runs down from the back of the braincase to the jaw joint. If the snake rests its head on the ground, ground vibrations are transmitted to the jaw and from it by way of the quadrate and stapes to the oval window. Physiological tests show that this leaves snakes much less sensitive than we are to airborne sounds, but much more sensitive to ground vibration. Their vibration sense must help them to detect the footsteps of approaching prey, or warn them of approaching enemies.

The snakes lost their eardrums in the course of evolution, but we mammals have retained ours, while slipping in an extraordinary complication. Instead of a single stapes connecting the eardrum to the oval window, we have a chain of three tiny bones, the ear ossicles, of which the innermost corresponds to the stapes of our reptile ancestors [PLATE 96]. The other two are the bones that formed the jaw joint in reptiles but became redundant in an astonishing series of changes in which the old jaw joint was replaced by a new one [PLATE 59].

PLATE 97

Skull of an air-breathing catfish.
Clarias sp.
The bony capsule for the
swimbladder is attached to the rear of
the skull, on the left of the picture.

PLATE 98

Skull of a Barn Owl.
Tyto alba
In some owl species the left and right
ears are asymmetrical, an arrangement
that improves the birds' ability to
locate sound sources.

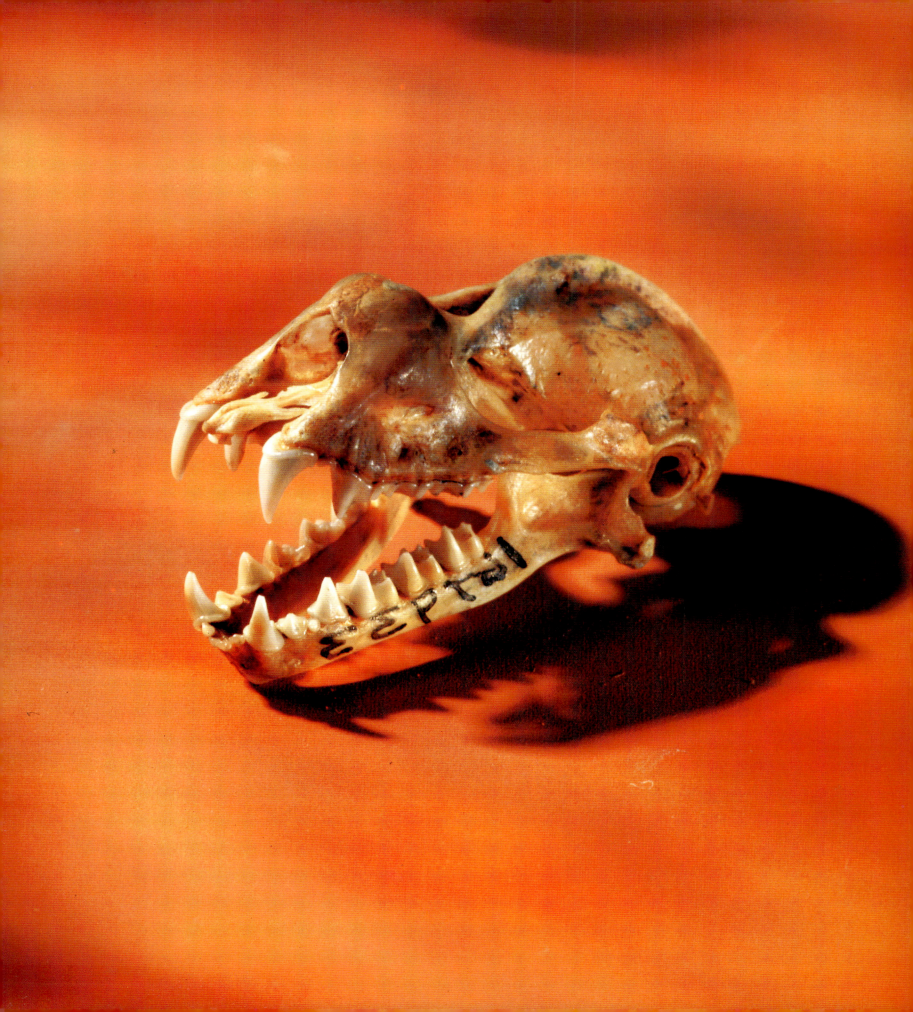

This asymmetry probably makes it easier for the owls to find the mice, voles and shrews that they eat. Owls hunt at night. Their big eyes [PLATE 98] collect what light there is, but when it is too dark for them to see well, rustling sounds from grass or fallen leaves may betray the presence of potential prey. If the owl can pinpoint the source of sound, it may get a meal.

When a sound source is to the left of my head, the sound reaches my left ear first. I depend partly on that, and partly on the sound being louder on the side nearer the source, to locate sources of sound. This effect, however, tells me only whether the sound comes from left or right, not whether it comes from below or above my head. The asymmetry of the owls' ears seems to overcome that problem. Experiments with a model of an owl's head showed that the asymmetry had much more effect on high-pitched sounds than on lower-pitched ones. The eardrums' responses to a lower-pitched sound show only whether the source is to the left or the right. Their responses to high frequency sound, however, show whether it is high up or low down. If the sound includes both high and low frequencies the owl can get full details of its direction, whether from left or from right and whether from high or low.

An owl depends on the sounds made by its prey but bats (which also hunt at night) find their insect prey by emitting high-pitched sounds and listening for echoes. This works particularly well when the insect as well as the bat is flying: if the insect is the only solid object near the bat, its echoes will be easier to pick out. Not only can the bat judge the direction of the insect, but it can also judge its distance by timing the interval between emitting the sound and hearing the echo. Sound travels through air at 330 meters (1080 feet) per second, so if the insect is 1 meter away a bat's cry takes $1/330 = .003$ seconds to reach it and the echo takes .003 seconds to get back to the bat, a total of .006 seconds. Similarly, you can estimate the distance of a thunderstorm by timing the interval between seeing the lightning and hearing the thunder. A 5 second interval, for instance, would indicate the lightning is approximately 1650 meters (or just over 1 mile) away.

The calls that bats use for echolocation are emitted mainly through the nostrils. One group of bats have an upward-pointing flap on the tip of the nose (looking rather like a third ear flap) which serves to direct the sound forward. A lump on the bones of the snout forms a base for this flap [PLATE 99].

Just as bats use airborne sounds to find insects, dolphins emit underwater sounds and find prey (fishes and squids) by echolocation. You may have noticed that the dolphin skull [PLATE 87] suggests a slender, pointed snout, but dolphins actually have bulging foreheads. The bulge is due to a pad of fat on top of the snout. This serves as a lens for the sound that the dolphin

PLATE 99

Skull of a Woolly Horseshoe Bat.
Rhinolophus luctus
The knob on the snout supported the nose flap that directed echo-location sounds forwards.

PLATE 100

Skull of a Desert Kangaroo Rat.
Dipodomys deserti
The swellings at the back of the skull
are the enlarged auditory bullae.

emits, directing it forward as a beam. Similarly, the lens of a flashlight focuses the light into a beam.

Good hearing is useful to predators finding prey, but prey with good hearing may be better able to escape the predators. Kangaroo rats are gerbil-sized rodents that live in the deserts of North America, hopping around on their hind legs like tiny kangaroos. They are wonderfully adapted for desert life. In laboratory tests, Professor Knut Schmidt-Nielsen of Duke University, North Carolina, found that he could keep them healthy on a diet of dry barley, with nothing at all to drink. In the desert, they avoid extreme heat by spending the day in burrows, coming to the surface to feed only during the cooler night. They have to dodge night-time predators such as owls which are hard to see in the dark, so good hearing is useful to them. Especially good hearing is needed to detect approaching owls because the soft edges of their feathers make their flight unusually quiet.

Look at the skull of the kangaroo rat [PLATE 100]. Those big swellings at the rear end are the tympanic bullae, the air-filled chambers containing the ear ossicles that connect the eardrum to the inner ear. Nearly all mammals have bullae, but they are usually little larger than is needed to contain the ossicles. In the small skulls of kangaroo rats the bullae are relatively huge.

A likely explanation is that they serve as resonators, making the ear exceptionally sensitive to certain sounds—including the sounds that owls' wings make as they move through the air. An air-filled cavity has a resonant frequency, and the air in it can very easily be set vibrating at that frequency: for example, you can produce a musical note by blowing across the top of an empty bottle, exciting its resonance.

Animals use the resonance of air-filled cavities in sound production as well as in hearing. One such resonator is a bony box that protrudes from a howler monkey's windpipe, at the top of the throat. Howler monkeys live high in the trees in South American rain forests. As their name suggests they emit howling cries, so loud that they can be heard 3 kilometers (2 miles) away through the forest. They move around in groups, feeding on fruit and leaves in the treetops. The groups hear each other's cries and keep away from one another, avoiding the fights that occur when groups accidentally meet.

Cranes also produce loud, raucous cries. Measurements in a zoo showed that the sound intensity of the call at a distance of 1 meter (39 inches) was in many cases more than 100 decibels: more, that is, than the sound intensity inside a rock band. Cranes and trumpeter swans (need I explain why they have that name?) have an anatomical oddity that seemed likely to help in the production of this appalling noise. Instead of running directly from mouth

to lungs, the windpipe enters the sternum (the plate of bone in the chest, to which the wing muscles attach) and coils around in it on its way to the lungs [PLATE 101]. Some crane species have windpipes more than twice as long as would be needed, if they ran straight.

People used to assume that the long windpipe served as a resonator, like an organ pipe or a trombone. Then Abbott Gaunt and his colleagues at Ohio State University pointed out that its length did not correspond to the pitch of the crane's call. A 1.2 meter (4 foot) organ pipe would sound at 150 cycles per second (if open at the end) or 75 cycles per second (if closed), but a crane with a windpipe that long produced a much higher-pitched call with a fundamental frequency of 770 cycles per second.

Gaunt and his colleagues performed a clever experiment to check that the pitch of the call did not depend on resonance of the windpipe. The resonant frequency of a gas-filled tube or cavity depends on the density of the gas: lighter gases give higher resonant frequencies. Helium is a low-density gas used (for that reason) to fill meteorological balloons. It is also used in deep-sea diving: by breathing an oxygen-helium mixture instead of air (which consists mainly of oxygen and nitrogen) divers avoid the ill effects of breathing nitrogen at high pressure, which can make them behave as if drunk. Divers breathing this mixture at the surface speak with squeaky voices because of the effect of the low-density helium on the resonant frequencies of the mouth and nasal cavities. Gaunt and his colleagues reasoned that if windpipe resonance was important for cranes, their calls would rise in pitch if they were given oxygen-helium to breathe. They tried, and found little effect. It seems that the pitch does not depend on windpipe resonance but (like the pitch of a human singer) on the resonance of the vocal chords, which can be tightened or slackened to give different notes.

Further experiments led to a different explanation for the over-long windpipe. The sternum probably acts as a sounding board, picking up vibrations from the windpipe and transmitting them to the air around the bird. Similarly, violins would make little noise if the strings were mounted on a solid rod instead of the conventional big, hollow body. The vibrations of the strings make the body vibrate, which acts on the surrounding air much more effectively than the strings alone could do.

With that background, we can speculate about the hollow crests on the skulls of some dinosaurs [PLATE 102]. The nasal passages which connect the nostrils (at the tip of the snout) to the back of the mouth cavity (where the windpipe starts) run all the way to the top of the crest and back, an unnecessarily long distance. *Lambeosaurus* (shown in the photograph) is remarkable but

PLATE 101

Sternum (breast bone) of a
Common Crane.
Grus grus
The windpipe is coiled within
the sternum.

PLATE 102

Skull of a crested hadrosaur.
Lambeosaurus lambei (Cretaceous period,
about 80 million years ago)
The crest may have functioned as a
resonator in voice production. This
skull is 82 centimeters (33 inches)
long.

a related dinosaur, *Parasaurolophus,* is extraordinary. Its crest projects one meter from the back of the skull. The nasal cavity is a connected pair of tubes that run from the nostrils, along the skull, up the crest and down again, a total distance (in some specimens) of more than three meters. David Weishampel of Johns Hopkins University believes that it served as a resonator, and used acoustic theory to reconstruct the dinosaur's song. We eliminated the crane windpipe as a resonator but the dinosaur suggestion seems plausible—it is unfortunate that we cannot test it by giving dinosaurs helium to breathe. The length of the nasal passages is about the same as that of a fully-extended trombone (measured along the folds of the tube, in both cases). Hence if the dinosaur matched its call to the resonance of the tube, its pitch would be close to the bottom of the trombone range, or about two octaves below middle C. Even if it did not, the long tube would affect the quality of the voice, giving it to an exaggerated degree the quality that distinguishes the voice of a human adult from that of a child.

The calculated pitch was for a really long-crested *Parasaurolophus.* Actually, the crests come in two size ranges, with the shorter ones only about half the length of the longer. The obvious inference is that the two length ranges represent two sexes; males with long crests and deep (or exaggeratedly "grown up" voices), and females with shorter crests and higher-pitched voices. The assumption that it is the males that have long crests comes from analogy with modern animals—the more ornamental animals are generally the males. In most species of duck, the males are brightly colored and the females dull brown. Peacocks are gorgeous blue and green with outsize tails while their females (peahens) are brown with short tails. Male hornbills have bigger ornaments on their bills than females [PLATE 103]. Stags have antlers but hinds (except of caribou) do not. Lions but not lionesses have manes.

Analogy with peacocks suggests further speculation. (The dinosaur crest does not look like an effective weapon, so seems more likely to have functioned as an ornament, like a peacock's tail, than to have been used for fighting like a stag's antlers.) Peacocks display their tails to females, who inspect the available talent and choose which male to mate with. Observations at Whipsnade Wild Animal Park in England showed that the longer-tailed males, with more spots on their tails, got nearly all the matings. It seems that peahens think long tails are sexy. Similarly, female *Parasaurolophus* probably preferred long-crested males. It can be shown theoretically that if a sexual preference like that (however irrational) starts to emerge in a population, the preference and the preferred male structure can evolve rapidly to extremes. The peacock's tail and the *Parasaurolophus* crest are certainly extreme.

There is a further twist in the dinosaur story that is not found in the peacock one. Some dinosaur species evolved solid crests, but the ancestors of *Parasaurolophus* happened to evolve their crests in a different way: the bones of the snout bulged upwards and backwards, carrying the nasal passages with them. This lengthened the passages, so gave the dinosaurs deeper (or more "grown up") voices. As a result, females came to associate deep (or more "grown up") voices with long sexy crests and the deep (or more "grown up") voice may in turn have become attractive to them. Female *Parasaurolophus* chose the males with the deepest bass voices. That may seem far fetched but it is biologically plausible—and you will find it hard to prove that it is wrong!

This chapter on acoustic functions of bones has been concerned (unsurprisingly) with consequences of the properties of sound. Sound does not pass easily from air to water so terrestrial animals have evolved eardrums and ear ossicles to assist the entry of sound to the fluid-filled inner ear. Sound makes bigger vibrations for the same pressure fluctuations in gases than in water, so some fishes have been able to use their swimbladders to amplify the sound signals reaching their ears. The resonance of air-filled chambers has been exploited in hearing by kangaroo rats and in sound production by howler monkeys and (probably) dinosaurs.

Another theme of the chapter has been changes of function in the course of evolution. We have seen bones from the jaw joint becoming ear ossicles, buoyancy organs becoming hearing aids, plates for wing muscle attachment becoming sounding boards and crests that may initially have been purely visual ornaments becoming sound producers as well. This theme of changing function will be developed further (alongside other themes) in the following chapter.

PLATE 103

Skull and bill of a Wrinkled
Hornbill.
Aceros corrugatus
The huge bill is a sexual ornament.

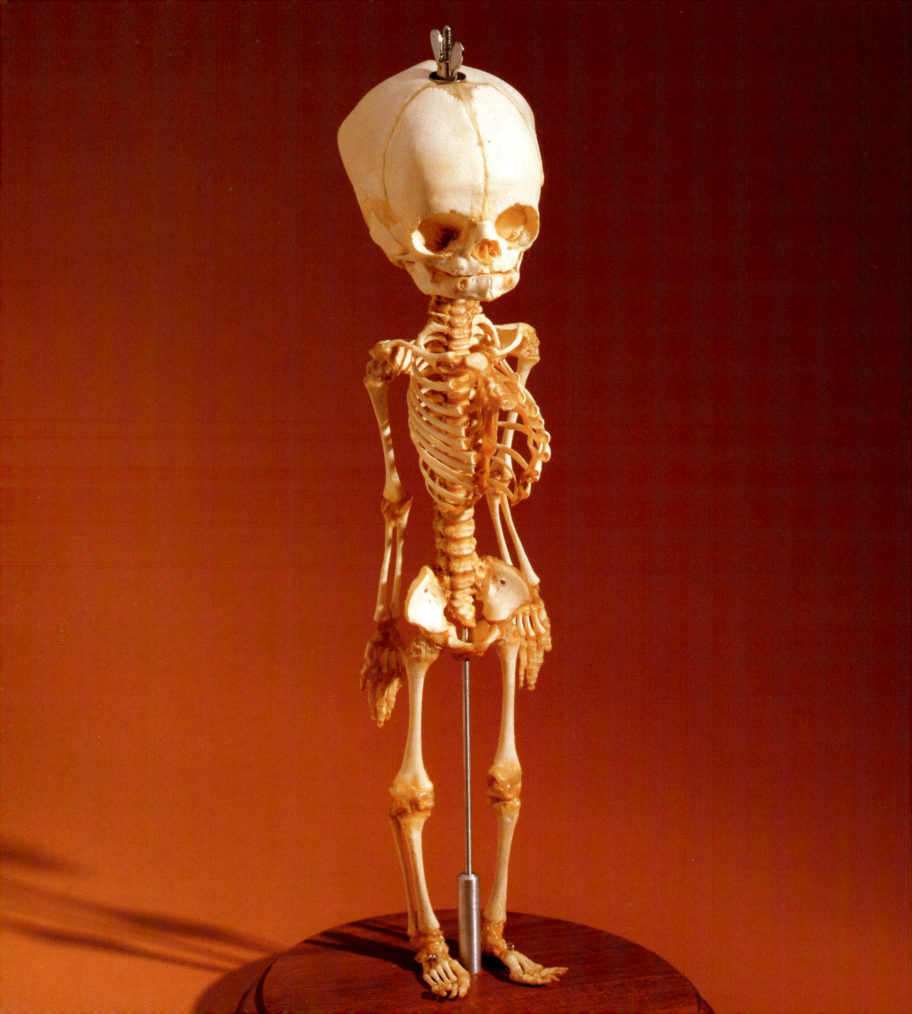

Chapter 8

DESIGNS THAT GROW

—————

THIS chapter is partly about how bones grow in the course of an animal's life, and partly about how bone design has developed in the course of evolution. In both cases, we will be thinking about problems that do not arise in conventional engineering. Bones have to be constructed, not only so that they can grow, but so as to function well at every stage of growth. In contrast, engineering structures are built to the required size and generally remain that size throughout their lives. Skeletons can evolve to new designs only by modifying existing ones, but an engineer who wants to build a new kind of structure can scrap the old design and start again from scratch.

We will think first about growth. Cells can grow by accumulating molecules which are fitted here and there into their structure, but the hard parts of bone can no more grow like that than you can enlarge your house by forcing new bricks here and there into the walls, in between the existing bricks. Bones can grow only by adding new bone to their surfaces or round the edges. Signs of this kind of growth can be seen when the scales of teleost fishes (which are made of bone) are examined under the microscope. It can be seen that the scale consists of a huge number of concentric rings of bone, each formed in a short spurt of growth. Fish grow faster in summer than in winter, so bands where the rings are closely spaced grew in winter and bands of more widely

PLATE 104

Skeleton of a human baby.
Homo sapiens
The proportions are quite different
from those of an adult.

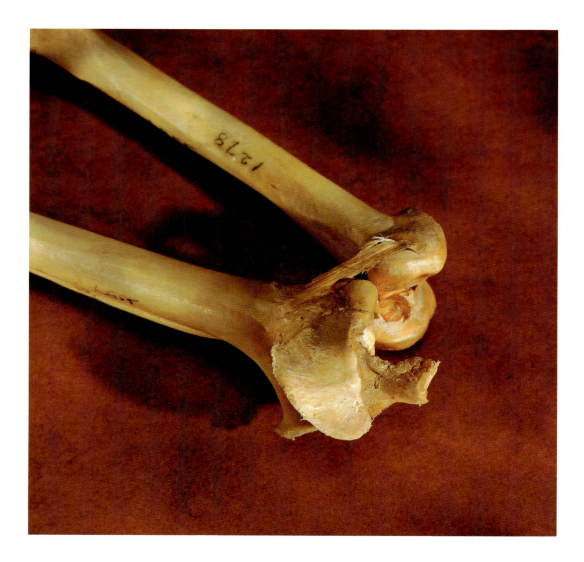

PLATE 106

Knee of a Wild Turkey.
Meleagris gallopavo
The tendon that connected the
kneecap to the tibia (shin bone)
is still in position.

the epiphyses fuse to the shaft to form a single mass of bone. In humans, this happens around age 18, providing one of the clues used by forensic scientists to judge the ages of skeletons. In young animals the epiphyses are still distinct [PLATE 58].

Epiphyses are found not only at joints, but also where some tendons attach to bones, for example on the heel at the attachment of the Achilles tendon [PLATE 105]. The olecranon process (funny bone) at the elbow, where the tendon of the triceps muscle attaches, is also a separate epiphysis in young mammals. Such traction epiphyses (as they are called) may have evolved from structures like the kneecap (called sesamoids). Compare the elbow with the knee. The tendon of the triceps muscle which extends the elbow attaches to the ulna (one of the forearm bones) by way of the epiphysis of the funny bone. We saw earlier how the quadriceps muscles which extend the knee attach to the tibia (shin bone) by means of a tendon which has a sesamoid (the kneecap) embedded in it [PLATE 106]. The essential difference between the funny bone and the kneecap is merely that the former is rigidly attached to the ulna by an epiphyseal plate while the latter is flexibly attached to the tibia by (in humans) about 2 centimeters (.8 inch) of tendon.

Stronger clues indicating the equivalence of traction epiphyses and sesamoids appear when birds are studied. Some birds have funny bones and kneecaps like mammals, but the elbows of swifts have sesamoids ("elbow caps") instead of epiphyses and the knees of the diving petrel have traction epiphyses instead of sesamoids. Use of one structure rather than the other in a particular joint may not be a matter of mere chance. Mathematical analysis shows that changing from a traction epiphysis to a sesamoid or the reverse may alter the mechanical advantage of the muscle.

Epiphyseal plates are points of weakness in bones, and sometimes split when children have accidents. The risk of damage is generally reduced by epiphyseal plates being bumpy: hills on the end of the bone shaft fit into hollows in the epiphysis, forming an interlocking joint.

Another problem of growth has been solved in the evolution of rodent teeth. Remember how rodent incisors (the front teeth, used for gnawing) grow continuously, so that what is lost by wear is replaced by growth. It is the tip of the crown that wears but the growth is at the base of the tooth, deep in its socket, so as it grows and wears the tooth has to be advanced in its socket, like the lead of a propelling pencil. This limits the range of possible tooth shapes. A straight tooth could be advanced in a straight socket, as straight leads can in straight pencils. A tooth that is curved into an arc of a circle can be advanced in a similarly curved socket, and rodent incisors are curved like

PLATE 108

Skull and horns of an Angora Goat.
Capra sp.
The horns are helical spirals,
like snail shells.

PLATE 107

Skull of a Nutria.
Myocastor coypus
About half the length of the upper
incisor tooth is visible, and half is
embedded in the skull.

PLATE 109

Lower jaw of a Crocodile.
Crocodylus sp.
Some of the bone has been cut away
to show developing teeth that would
have replaced the ones currently in
use, when they were shed.

that. The upper incisor [PLATE 107], including the part hidden in the socket, forms an almost complete semicircle. A semicircular tooth can be advanced but a spiral, wavy or parabolic one would be jammed, unable to move, in a close-fitting socket.

A helical (corkscrew-shaped) arc is an alternative solution to the same problem, and the tusks of mammoths (another example of a continuously growing tooth in a deep socket) were helical.

Another beautiful class of shape, which seems to have been evolved for reasons of growth, are horns. The horns of rams and the Angora goat [PLATE 108] are helical spirals, corkscrews whose coils become progressively tighter toward the point. The same class of shapes is also seen in snail shells—possibly for the same reason, for horns and snail shells have something important in common.

Snail shells and nautilus shells [PLATE 16] grow by adding material around the opening. Horns are not living bone, but dead keratin. The Angora goat has a core of bone in its horns, as the picture shows, but this core does not reach far up the horn: the bulk of the horn (and all the visible part) is keratin, the material of hooves, fingernails and hair. Keratin cannot be added to the outer surface of the horn because there is no living tissue there, but only at the base where it meets the bony core.

The special property of helical spirals like Angora goat horns and snail shells is that they can be enlarged by adding material at one end, without changing their shape. If you add material to one end of a cylindrical rod without increasing its diameter proportionately, the resulting rod is not only longer but also relatively more slender: the ratio of diameter to length is reduced. Adding to a snail shell, however, makes it bigger without changing its proportions. The same is true of cones (like limpet shells, and the straight horns of some antelopes) but a cone is simply a snail-shell shape without the curves.

Rodent incisors and elephant tusks grow continuously, but most teeth stop growing when they come into use. That presents a problem because growing animals need bigger teeth as their mouths get bigger. A 25-centimeter (10-inch) crocodile hatchling may grow to a 5-meter (16-foot) adult, but would have trouble fitting even one of the adult's teeth into its tiny mouth. Fortunately, it does not have to start its life with grown-up teeth. As it grows, it sheds small teeth and replaces them with larger ones, new teeth forming under the old ones they would replace [PLATE 109]. The old teeth are not shed all at once (that would leave a toothless and hungry crocodile) but by turns according to a complicated pattern. The teeth being changed at any

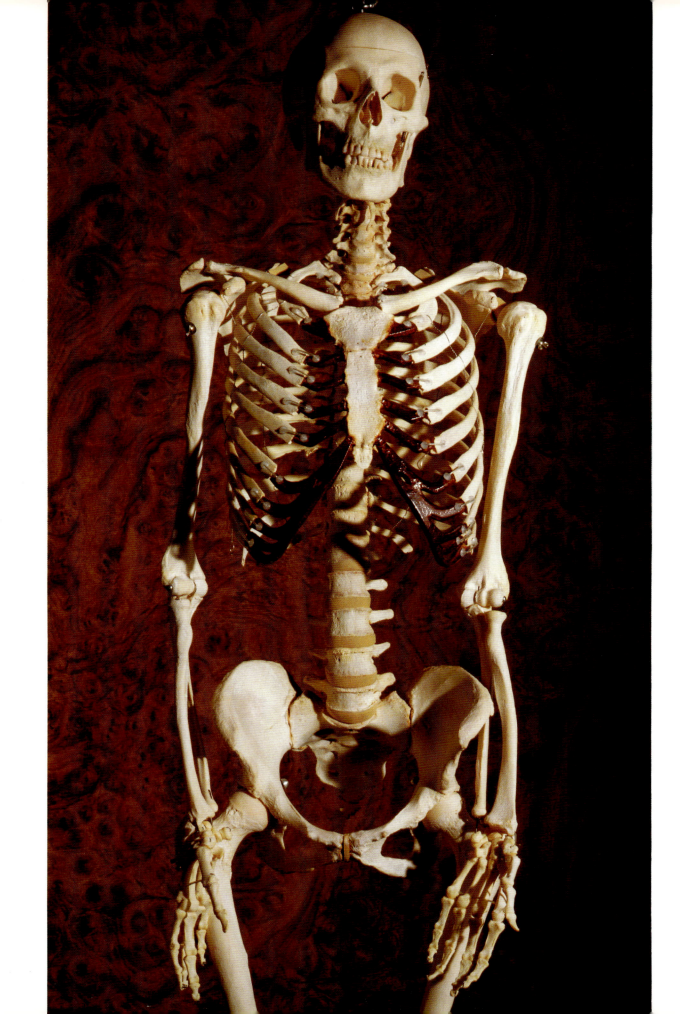

time are scattered around the jaws, and no part of the jaws is ever seriously short of teeth.

A crocodile needs many replacement sets of teeth in the course of its life, but we mammals make do with only one, when we lose and replace our milk teeth. We can make do with only two sets of teeth because our size changes less dramatically during growth than the sizes of reptiles do, and in any case we need no teeth while suckling so we have grown a lot before our first teeth appear.

Unlike snails' shells, many bones do not keep their proportions constant as they grow. For example, a human baby's skull is quite different in shape from the skull of an adult: the baby's face is short and its braincase relatively very large. A baby's limbs are remarkably short, relative to the length of the back. A baby is by no means a scale model of an adult [PLATES 104 and 110].

Such differences in proportions between different-sized individuals can be seen in comparisons between species, as well as between growth stages of a single species. A particularly good comparison is between a lion and a domestic cat [PLATE 36], because these are closely related animals of very different sizes. In many respects, a typical cat is close to being a quarter-scale model of a lion. It is about 25 centimeters (10 inches) tall at the shoulder compared to the lion's 1 meter (almost 40 inches). Its leg bones are all about one quarter the length of the corresponding lion bones. If it were an exact quarter scale model of the lion, the lion would be four times as long, four times as wide and four times as high as the cat and would have 4 x 4 x 4 = 64 times the cat's volume. Because cats and lions are made of similar materials this implies that the lion would have 64 times the mass of the cat, which is about right: a typical cat has a mass of about 2.5 kilograms (6 pounds) and a typical lion about 160 kilograms (360 pounds).

Despite this similarity you would never mistake an enlarged photograph of a cat (even a cat without stripes) for a photograph of a lioness. Part of the reason is that cats have relatively much larger eyes, .4% of body mass compared to .04% for a lion. The eye socket [PLATE 111] is relatively much larger even in a bobcat (much larger than a domestic cat) than in a lion. It also shows that the braincase, behind the eyes, is much more swollen in the bobcat than the lion, corresponding to the smaller cat's relatively larger brain (1.1% of body mass in domestic cats compared to .2% in lions). Similar differences of eye and brain proportions are seen whenever related animals of very different sizes are compared. They are shown as clearly by reptiles as by mammals [PLATE 112], and are responsible for the popular belief that dinosaurs had tiny brains. The space for the brain in large dinosaur skulls

PLATE 110

Skeleton of an adult human.
Homo sapiens

shows that brain mass must have been a tiny fraction of body mass (50 ton brachiosaurs had 200-gram or 7-ounce brains). Modern reptiles, however, have much smaller brains than mammals, and if you calculate the expected sizes for dinosaur brains by scaling up from present-day reptiles, allowing for the changes in proportions with body size that are seen in modern animals, it turns out that dinosaurs had brains of about the sizes expected for reptiles with their body masses.

The explanation for these changes of proportions seems to be that animals of different sizes are generally built of similar-sized cells: cat cells are about the same size as lion cells. This implies that larger animals have more cells in their bodies, which has consequences for the functioning of eyes and brains.

The fineness of detail that an eye can see depends on the number of sense cells in the retina: the more cells, the better the visual acuity. If a lion had eyes exactly the same size as a cat it could see as well as a cat. With its bigger eyes (absolutely bigger, though relatively smaller) it can presumably see more detail than the cat. The larger size of the lion's head enables it to fit in a bigger, better eye, but there is no reason to expect the eye to become as big, relative to the body, as do the eyes of cats. Similarly, lion brains contain many more cells than do the smaller brains of cats, so are presumably capable of more complicated operations (of assimilating more information from sense organs, or of controlling more complex behavior), but there is no apparent need for a lion's brain to be as big, relative to the body, as is the brain of a cat.

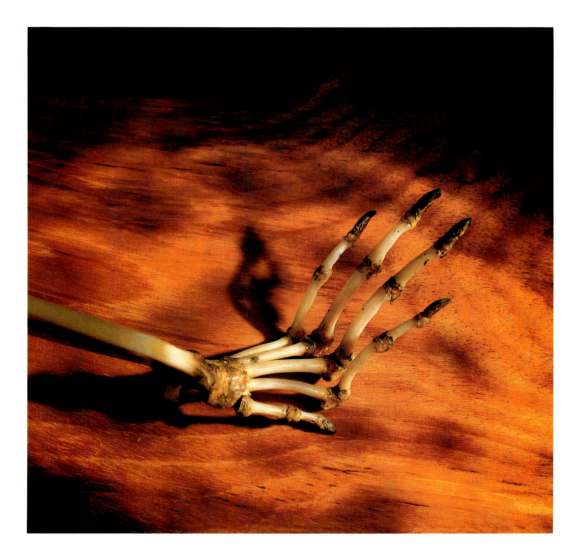

PLATE 114

Hand skeleton of a White-throated
Capuchin Monkey.
Cebus capucinus

We have seen how bones grow and how the proportions of the skeleton change with changing body size, whether comparisons are made between growth stages of one species or between adults of related species of contrasting size. We will finish the chapter by looking at problems not of growth but of evolution.

Biologists tend to think of evolution as the perfect design process, particularly powerful because it proceeds automatically without the need for any designer to think up new ideas. However, it has the severe disadvantage that we have already noticed: it cannot scrap a design and start afresh, but can only advance by tinkering with existing designs.

You can see evolutionary tinkering in a small way, in the hands of primates. The capuchin monkey [PLATE 114] has typical monkey hands. The orangutan [PLATE 115] has long fingers, good for hooking over branches, and short thumbs that will not get in the way as it swings through the trees. And the Madagascan Aye-aye [PLATE 116] has immensely long, thin middle fingers for extracting insect larvae from their burrows in dead branches.

There has been more drastic tinkering with the basic design in the evolution of the horse's foot [PLATE 117]. This has become lighter, making fast running easier, by reducing the number of toes. The single strong toe with the hoof on its end is the equivalent of the middle finger of the human hand. On either side it has a sliver of bone, too thin and weak to serve any useful function that I can think of. These are the remnants of the toes corresponding to the index and ring fingers. They seem not to be there to do any job, but only because evolution has failed to complete the job of eliminating them. The side toes of kangaroos are also reduced [PLATE 118].

The whale's skull [PLATE 119] also reveals its history. Other mammals have their nostrils at the tip of the snout, but whales have theirs on the top of the head, which makes it easier for them to take in air when they come to the surface to breathe. An engineer producing a new-design skull with nostrils on the top of the head would simply omit making the old-style nostrils, and cut out new ones in the new position. Evolution, however, can advance only by modifying existing designs gradually, keeping them working at all stages in the transition. Let us see how it did this particular job.

The nostrils of mammals are framed by two pairs of bones, the premaxillae below and the nasals above. The premaxillae are the bones that hold the front teeth of the upper jaw, and the nasal bones form the roof of the nasal cavity, extending back along the roof of the skull from the nostrils to near the eye sockets. The engineer's obvious way to change the position of the nostrils would be simply to perforate the skull behind the nasal bones, instead of in

PLATE 115

Hand skeleton of an Orangutan.
Pongo pygmaeus
The fingers are long and the
thumb short.

PLATE 116

Skeleton of an Aye-aye.
Daubentonia madagascariensis
All the fingers are long. The very
slender middle finger, which is
the longest, is used for extracting
insect larvae from their burrows
in dead branches.

PLATE 117

Skeleton of a horse's foot.
Equus caballus
The heel is on the right and the hoof
out of the picture on the left. The
thin slivers of bone on either side of
the stout cannon bone are rudiments
of lost toes.

PLATE 118

Skeleton of a Grey Kangaroo foot.
Macropus giganteus
The long, strong toe is the
fourth one.

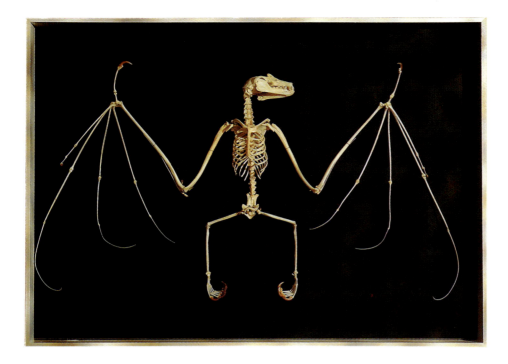

surface is an extension of the skin, stretched between the limbs (especially the long fingers) and the body [PLATE 121]. The extinct pterosaurs evolved their wings in another way, again using a flap of skin but supporting it with just one enormously enlarged finger [PLATE 20]. The small wings of flying squirrels are flaps of skin stretched between the fore and hind legs, with added support given by an elongated, spur-like wrist bone [PLATE 120]. Here are four strikingly different ways of modifying existing limbs to make wings. In each case, every bone in the wing can be recognized as having evolved from a particular leg bone possessed by running ancestors, and in no case have wings been produced by adding extra limbs. It is almost inconceivable that evolution should produce ordinary angels, let alone the fancier sorts such as cherubim which are said to have three pairs of wings.

This chapter has shown how bones grow by adding new material on the outside and by eating bone away to enlarge cavities, and how epiphyses allow growth without disruption of joints. It has suggested reasons why some teeth grow in the shape of arcs of circles and why the horns of Angora goats are coiled like snail shells. We have discussed why lions and cats have differently shaped skulls and why the proportions of moose leg bones are not more different from those of mouse deer. We have seen how evolution's dependence on change by successive small modifications of existing structures has left horses with useless side toes and whales with strangely distorted snouts. Finally, we have deplored evolution's inability to produce angels.

Chapter 9

PATTERNS AND TEXTURES

P REVIOUS chapters have looked at bone from an engineering point of view, trying to relate structure to function. We have seen how bones are built to combine strength with lightness; how joints are shaped to allow some movements and prevent others; how bones are in some cases jointed together to form complex mechanisms; how teeth are adapted for gripping, cutting or grinding; and how tiny bones in our ears make us sensitive to sound. By applying different branches of engineering we have been able to explain many aspects of bone structure. We have seen that, to a very large extent, skeletons are built as they are for good functional reasons.

In Chapter 8, however, hints began to appear that life might not always be so logical. We found splint bones in the feet of horses which seem to be there, not because they serve any useful function (they seem to be utterly useless), but because horses evolved from ancestors that had and used more than one toe. We saw that however desirable it might be to retain arms while evolving wings, angel-like animals would be most unlikely to evolve because legged vertebrates have no more than two pairs of limbs. When birds, bats and pterosaurs evolved wings, they did so by modifying their forelegs, which became much less effective (or even unusable) as legs. Evolution can operate only by tinkering with existing designs so its course is constrained by past evolutionary history. Function is not by itself sufficient to explain the structure of skeletons.

PLATE 122

Skull of a fossil amphibian. *Trematops* (Permian period, about 270 million years ago)

PLATE 123

Skull of another fossil amphibian.
Trematosaurus branuni (Triassic period,
about 220 million years ago)

In this chapter on patterns and textures we will find some beautiful examples of structure adapted to function. We will also find structures that seem to be to a large extent accidental, at least in their details. These apparently accidental details are extremely helpful to systematists in their attempts to work out the relationships between groups of animals, and to trace the course of evolution: the more similar animals are in functionally insignificant details, the more closely they are likely to be related.

We will start by looking at some fossil skulls. Bony skulls are never formed in one piece but are built up from plates of bone, sutured together. A skull built from separate plates may be weaker than a one-piece skull would be, but it can grow more economically. A one-piece skull could grow only by adding new bone on the outside while enlarging the cavity inside by eating away old bone, as happens when leg bones grow. A skull composed of many separate bony plates, however, can grow mainly by thickening the plates and adding bone around their edges, with very little need for the presumably costly process of eating bone away and replacing it. This argument suggests a functional reason for having the skull built up from many independent bones, but tells us nothing about how those bones should be arranged. Many different patterns of plates would be possible, and there may be a large number of alternative patterns that would all be more or less equally satisfactory. The pattern found in an animal may depend more on its ancestry than on function, and different patterns may have been adopted by different animal groups purely by chance.

Very often we find well-defined patterns repeated time and again in groups of related animals with very little variation. The pattern of bones in the skulls of the early amphibians, the first land-living vertebrates, is a good example. The rough surfaces of the bones often make it difficult to see the hair-thin joints between one bone and the next, especially in imperfectly preserved fossils [PLATE 122], so instead of looking at photographs we will look at diagrams in which the joints have been marked conspicuously, after long and careful study of the original fossils.

To see the basic pattern of the skull roof look first at *Trematosaurus* [FIGURE M, *left;* also PLATE 123], the fossil of an animal that lived 220 million years ago. Some holes in the skull will serve as landmarks: the nostrils near the tip of the snout, the larger eye sockets farther back, and the single small hole in the center line, near the back of the skull. This last housed the pineal eye, a light-sensitive organ, capable of detecting light but not of forming images, which is present in many vertebrates (including ourselves) though often roofed-over by bone. The pineal eye senses the daily rhythm of light and darkness, matching

PLATE 125

Fossil of an early lungfish.
Scaumenacia (Devonian period,
about 380 million years ago)

kinds of fin found in most modern fishes. The earliest fossil amphibians retain a finny edge to the tail and a tiny remnant of a fish-like gill cover, but the pattern of skull bones gives the clearest indication of relationship between the amphibians and this group of fishes.

Consideration of another fish will help us to appreciate the force of this argument. *Scaumenacia*, an early lung fish, lived at the same time as *Eusthenopteron* and look superficially similar [PLATE 125]. It was fairly similar in shape (though with a differently shaped tail), with similar scales and similar fleshy fins. However, its skull pattern was quite different, so different that it seems impossible to identify corresponding bones. It seems likely that the common ancestor of these two fishes had a skull formed from a very large number of small bones which joined together in different groupings to evolve the two patterns.

The Weberian ossicles that help some fish to hear provide another example of details of pattern helping us to spot evolutionary relationships. We saw in Chapter 7 that they are found in all the members of the Ostariophysi, including the characins, catfishes, carps and electric eels. The characins include the fearsome piranha but are for the most part fairly ordinary-looking fish. Many of the catfishes look bizarre with flattened bodies, small eyes, long barbels (feelers) and formidable defensive spines. Electric eels are distinguished by the electric organs that are the basis of their remarkable electric sense. If it were not for the Weberian ossicles, there would be hardly anything to make us group these very diverse fishes together. However, they all have Weberian ossicles (which no other fishes have) and there is remarkable consistency in the structure of the system. In every case, it is formed by the same parts of the first three vertebrae and of the third pair of ribs. The similarities extend to trivial details that seem unlikely to affect function: for example, I can see no reason why a system built from two vertebrae instead of three should not work as well. It seems grossly unlikely that if the swimbladder-ear connection had been evolved independently in different groups of fish it would have taken so precisely the same form in each case. (We saw in Chapter 8 that although forelegs were modified to form wings in the evolution of birds, bats and pterosaurs, the details came out quite differently in the three cases.) Zoologists are convinced that the Weberian apparatus can have evolved only once, in some group that was ancestral to characins, catfishes, carps and electric eels.

Striking similarities of pattern are also found between successive parts of the skeleton. Look at the highly regular, repeating pattern in the fin skeleton of a fish with similar supports under each fin ray, and one vertebra very much

like the next [PLATES 50 and 126]. Similar repetition is found in structures built by humans. For example, an engineer building a bridge may design it as a series of identical modules which are bolted together to make the complete structure. In fishes, successive modules (vertebrae or fin ray supports) may not be quite identical, but they are plainly constructed according to the same plan.

This kind of construction needs less genetic information to provide the instructions for development than a structure in which every part is quite different from the next. Similarly, an engineer building a modular bridge would need detailed drawings of only one module. We do not know much about how the instructions for developing vertebrae are inherited by fish from their parents, but the principles are probably the same as for the development of the segments of fruit flies (the geneticists' favorite animal for studying questions of this kind).

The bodies of fruit flies, like those of all other insects, consist of a series of segments, one behind another. The three pairs of legs, each very like the next, develop on three successive segments. Behind them, the abdomen consists of a series of segments, each protected above and below by its own plates of cuticle—the black stripes on a wasp mark the boundaries between segments. Geneticists have learned a great deal about how this segmentation is controlled by observing what goes wrong when a mutation changes one of the

genes. They have discovered that there are segmentation genes that decide the number of segments: a mutation in one of these, for example, may make the embryo start developing with only half the normal number of segments. There are other genes that have the same effect on each of a succession of segments, for example controlling the shapes of the rear edges of all the segments of the abdomen. And there are genes that are responsible for differences between segments: a mutation in one example among these makes legs instead of antennae develop on the fruit fly's head. Thus there are genes to say how many modules there should be, others to say what the modules in general should be like and yet others to specify particular features of individual modules. Such a system enables a reasonably small number of genes to carry the instructions for building a body with a large number of distinct parts. The genes involved were first studied in fruit flies, but later research has discovered similar genes in other animals.

Vertebral columns and fins are single lines of modules, but the scales of fishes make repeating patterns in two dimensions on the surface of the skin [PLATE 127]. The bichir, a primitive African fish, has square bony scales that fit neatly edge to edge and form a protective armor over the whole body. Very few modern fishes have scales like this, but such scales were common in the early days of the bony fishes, 400 million years ago. The lines of scales run obliquely down from the middle of the back to the middle of the belly, each line forming a half turn of a corkscrew curve as it wraps round the body.

Most modern fishes have a much lighter covering of paper-thin scales, which are also made of bone. The corkscrew pattern is evident also in their arrangement: you can follow lines of scales running obliquely downward and backward, and others running obliquely upward and backward. This arrangement corresponds to the pattern of fibers (of the protein collagen) in the fish's skin, a fabric of fibers running obliquely in these two directions. This is the best arrangement of fibers for skin that has to allow the tail to bend freely from side to side as the fish swims.

The roof of my house is covered with tiles which overlap so that everywhere there is one tile on top of another: that arrangement is much more weather-proof than if the tiles formed a single layer, meeting edge-to-edge. The scales of many fishes overlap even more, so that every part of the body is covered by three overlapping scales. Weatherproofing is not an issue here, but the thinness of the scales makes them flexible and three layers give more protection than a single layer (of scales of the same thickness) would give. Thus the overlapping arrangement may have evolved as a good way of building flexible armor. However, there is another advantage that follows from the three-fold overlap.

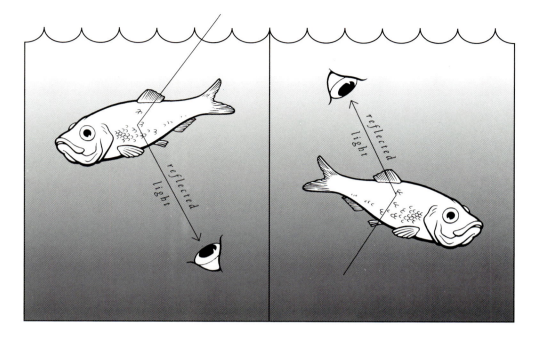

FIGURE N

A silvery fish seen from above in the sea looks dark and is seen against a dark background, but seen from below it looks bright against a bright background.

Thin bony scales are transparent, but many fish such as herrings have mirrors on the undersides of their scales that reflect light, giving them their silvery appearance. The reflections from the silvery fish in a fishmonger's shop may catch your eye, but when the fish are swimming in their natural habitat, the silveriness is effective camouflage. A silvery fish viewed obliquely from below is seen against the bright background of the sky, and the scales on its sides reflect the bright light of the sky into the observer's eye, so the fish looks bright against a bright background [FIGURE N]. The same fish viewed from above is seen against the dark background of the depths, and its sides reflect dim light from the dark depths, so it looks dark against a dark background. In either case the fish is inconspicuous. The mirrors are not tiny versions of the ones we have in our bathrooms, which reflect all colors of light equally. Instead, they are interference mirrors, like the mirrors that make some beetles iridescent. Different interference mirrors are needed to reflect different colors, and the reflected color changes with the angle of the light—that is why the color of an iridescent beetle changes as you turn it. The light deep in the sea is mainly blue, but a fish may be seen from any direction so needs mirrors that will reflect blue light coming from any direction if it is to be camouflaged satisfactorily. The overlap of the scales enables the fish to have several sets of mirrors superimposed. Different parts of each silvery scale have mirrors that will reflect blue light coming from different directions, and the overlap is arranged so that these different kinds of mirrors are superimposed. If light is

PLATE 128

Shell of a Starred Tortoise.
Psammobates tentorius
The sutures between the bones do
not coincide with the edges of the
horny scales.

not reflected by the mirrors of the topmost scale, it will pass through and be reflected by a deeper scale. Thus the overlapping pattern of the scales seems to be useful in an unexpected way.

The pattern of the horny scales on a tortoise shell is more complex than that of the bony scales of fishes: these scales are not simply arranged in diagonal lines. When most of the horny scales have been removed from the tortoise shell [PLATE 128], their pattern remains visible, as an impression in the underlying bone. Each horny plate had a pattern of concentric ridges on it, marking the stages of its growth, and this pattern became impressed on the growing bone. You might expect that the pattern of horny scales would match the pattern of the bones but this is not the case: each horny plate partly covers at least two bony ones. The photograph shows that the sutures where the bones meet (visible as fine lines) do not run around the outlines of the impressions of the horny plates but often run down their middles.

We turn now from patterns formed by complete bones, to the much finer patterns of roughness on the surfaces of individual bones. Look at the contrasting textures of an alligator skull [PLATE 129], rough where the bone is embedded in the skin and smooth where there are muscles or other tissues between it and the skin. Look also at the giraffe skull, rough under the central knob on the forehead and smooth elsewhere [PLATE 130].

PLATE 129

American Alligator skull.
Alligator mississippiensis
Bones that lie immediately under
the skin are rough but those that lie
deeper are smooth.

PLATE 130

Giraffe skull.
Giraffa camelopardalis
The rough bone of the knob on the
skull roof contrasts with smooth bone
on the sides.

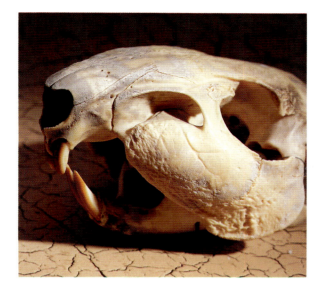

There are interesting textures also on the skull of the paca, a South American rodent with a remarkably large cheek bone [PLATE 131]. This cheekbone lies close under the skin and has a rough surface, but it is also marked by a Y-shaped groove. I have never had an opportunity to dissect a paca so I cannot be sure why the groove is there, but comparison with a guinea pig (a close relative) convinces me that a branch of the infraorbital artery (a small artery that takes blood to the cheek) must have lain in the groove. At the front end of the cheek bone there is a deep notch through which very smooth bone can be seen. Smooth bone is appropriate here, where a jaw muscle rubbed against it.

We started this chapter by looking at the arrangement of individual bones within skeletons. We found patterns whose details seemed to depend more on accidents of ancestry than on function, in the skulls of amphibians and in the Weberian ossicles of fishes. We saw how such patterns can help systematists by providing clues about evolutionary relationships. Next we looked at repeating patterns in the skeletons of fishes, seeing how their fins and backbones are built from a row of similar modules. Experiments on fruit flies suggested simple but effective genetic mechanisms that might control the inheritance of such patterns. After that, we looked at the patterns of fish scales and saw how the diagonal rows of scales reflected the pattern of fibers in the underlying skin, and how mirrors on overlapping scales serve as camouflage. Then we saw how the textures of bone surfaces can tell us about the soft tissues that overlay them, in the living animal.

Finally, we will look at just one more pattern, the wiggly line of the suture between bones in a human skull [PLATE 132]. The interlocking wiggles make

PLATE 133

Skull of a Bush Pig.
Potamochoerus porcus
The sutures are much straighter than
in the roof of a human skull.

the joint stronger than it would be if the bones simply met edge to edge,
like some of the bones in a Bush Pig skull [PLATE 133], but they present an
intriguing puzzle: how long is the wiggly suture? The question is not as easy
as it sounds.

You could measure the suture by laying a ruler along it, measuring the
straight-line distance between its ends. Alternatively you could lay a thread
along the suture, following the wiggles as closely as you could, and then
straighten the thread out and measure it. That way you would measure the
wiggly path and get a longer length. Even using that method you could follow
only the larger wiggles, and, if you could devise a method of following all the
wiggles shown in the photograph, you would get an even longer length, about
three times the straight line length. You might claim that that was the true
length, but, if you used a microscope to obtain a magnified photograph, you
would see finer wiggles and be able to measure a longer length. At each level
of increased magnification still more wiggles would be visible. We have to
conclude that there is no such thing as the length of such a suture. Instead
we could, if we wanted, measure a quantity designed to cope with such awkward situations called fractal extent. This concept comes from the branch
of mathematics called fractal geometry, which has become widely known for
the beautiful patterns it can generate on computer screens. Here is a possible
application of a bright young branch of mathematics to the old (but still
lively) subject of anatomy.

PLATE 132

The roof of a human skull.
Homo sapiens
The sutures wiggle like a coastline
in a map.

Chapter 10

EPILOGUE:
FUNCTION and BEAUTY

IN this book we have looked at many different bones taken from animals ranging from fish to mammals. Sometimes we have looked at whole skeletons and sometimes at individual bones, and these bones have come from all parts of the body. We have used these many bones to illustrate a wide range of topics, exploring in each chapter a different aspect of bone design. In this last short chapter I will recapitulate the topics and show how they can all be illustrated by a single skull. I have chosen the skull of an eagle because it is, to me, one of the most striking and beautiful objects in any museum [PLATE 134].

First we discussed the strength of bones, showing by many examples how skeletons combine strength with lightness. The eagle's beak is formidably strong where strength is needed, but some other parts of the skull are remarkably delicate. Even the strong upper jaw is very light, built like a box girder of plates of bone enclosing an empty, air-filled space. The skull roof, too, is lightly built. If we cut it open we would find that it was a sandwich structure, made of two sheets of compact bone separated by a spongy layer. In mammals the pores of the sponge would be filled with marrow but in the eagle they are filled with air, making the bones much lighter.

In the next chapter, we discussed joints. Look at the jaw joint of the eagle [PLATE 135]: on each side of the head, two knobs on one of the skull bones

PLATE 134

Skull of a Bald Eagle.
Haliaeetus leucocephalus

PLATE 137

The ear region of the
Bald Eagle's skull.
Haliaeetus leucocephalus

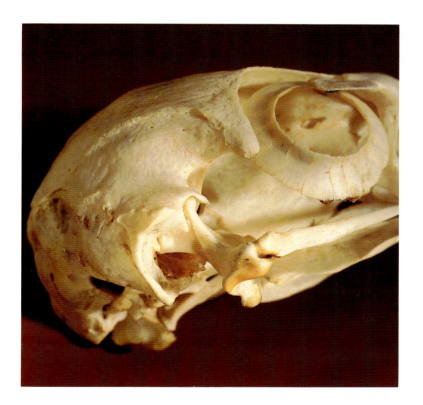

PLATE 138

The bones that reinforce the
Bald Eagle's eyeball.
Haliaeetus leucocephalus

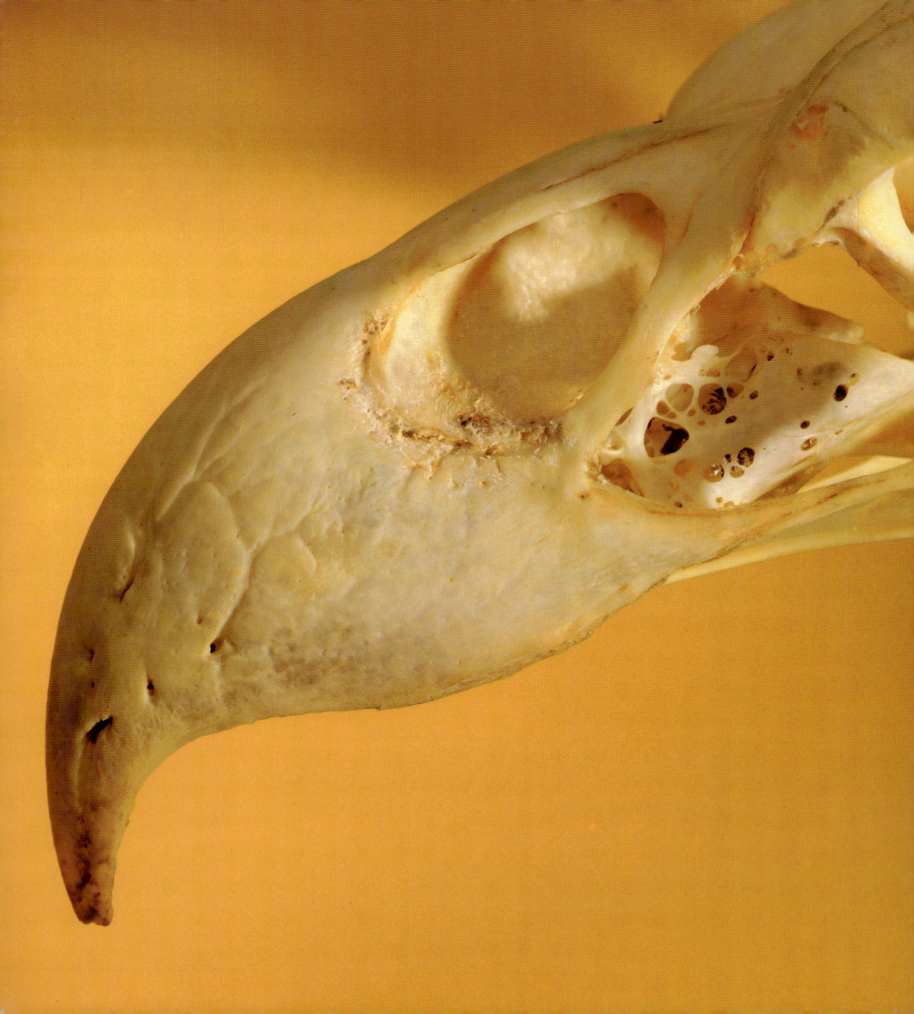

between the braincase and the upper jaw there is a flexible strip of bone that has to bend to allow the upper jaw to be tilted [PLATE 134].

The next chapter was about teeth. The eagle of course has none, but has instead a horny covering on the jaws, forming a sharp-edged beak. The point is well adapted for piercing the skin of the prey which can then be torn by the hook-like beak.

Acoustic bones were the subject of Chapter 7. We were concerned largely with the eardrum and ear ossicles, which ensure that as much sound energy as possible enters the ear and as little as possible is reflected. We mammals have external ears that funnel sound in to the eardrum but birds (like amphibians and reptiles) do not. Their eardrum lies close behind the jaw joint, where it is hidden by feathers, but the arrangement of eardrum and stapes in the eagle [PLATE 137] is essentially the same as in frogs [PLATE 94].

Chapter 8 was about the growth of bones and also about how evolution has to work, by tinkering with existing designs rather than starting afresh with new ones. A ring of small plates of bone is embedded in the bird's huge eyeball [PLATE 138]. A one-piece ring would make more effective reinforcement but this ring consists of many separate bones, an arrangement that presumably reduces the cost of growth. A continuous ring would have to grow by adding new bone to its circumference and removing bone from the inner edge. If this were the case, the total quantity of bone produced as the hatchling grew to adult size would be considerably more than remains in the eye of the adult. Because the ring consists of separate plates it can grow by addition of bone along the edges of the plates (including the edges where one plate meets the next), with little or no need to remove any of the old bone.

Finally, in Chapter 9 we examined patterns and textures. The ring that we have just looked at presents a striking pattern. Look also at the texture of the bone of the beak, where it was covered in life by horn [PLATE 139]. The tiny holes and grooves carried the blood vessels that nourished the horn, and the nerves that gave the beak its sensitivity.

Last of all, I would like to say explicitly something that is implicit in the whole concept of this illustrated book. Bones are not only the marvels of engineering design that I have emphasized in my text. They are also the beautiful objects that Brian Kosoff's photographs have shown them to be. We hope that you will enjoy them in both ways.

PLATE 139

The Bald Eagle's bill.
Haliaeetus leucocephalus

PLATE 140

Bald Eagle.
Haliaeetus leucocephalus

Photographer's Statement

In the course of my 15 years as a professional photographer, I have, on occasion, photographed some unusual subjects. But I had little preparation when I was asked to produce 140 photographs of bones. "Why bones?" I thought. It took months for me to answer that question.

At first I was somewhat uneasy handling the specimens. After all, these "items" were previously inside something. Something that was alive. I wasn't sure if my uneasiness was from the fact that these were formerly inside an animal or that these bones represented death.

Later I grew accustomed to handling bones and became very familiar with them. I found myself fascinated by them. They were all so different, so specialized. It was amazing that so many different shapes and textures could come from the same basic material and serve the same basic purposes, that something so hard could grow so exactly within a living body. The design of these specimens would surely make an engineer envious. But there was something else to them, something powerful. They were the sole physical remnants of a living creature.

The power of these bones became amplified to me the first time I photographed human remains. Here was the skull of a person. I tried hard to deduce if it was male or female, the age at which this person died, where it came from. And, was this person alive during my lifetime? That question held tremendous emotion for me. Because, if this person coexisted with me, there is a chance, although very remote, that this was someone I might have known. This thought was most disturbing to me, and, although I treated all of the specimens carefully, I had some instinctive reverence for the human bones.

That reverence was most apparent when I photographed the skeleton of a stillborn child. There is always something tragic about the death of a helpless and innocent child. My publisher felt that this "specimen" might provoke strong feelings and forewarned me of its delivery. There is very little that a person unaccustomed to this sort of thing can do to prepare for the presence of such an object. It stood only 20 inches high, the sutures of its skull still unclosed. The delicateness of its hands was quite moving. This was some parents' hope for the future.

It wasn't, though, only the presence of human bones that evoked in me strong emotions. I remember photographing the warthog skull. This skull had several large holes which went clean through its thick bone. I assumed this damage occurred during the shipping of this specimen. I later learned that these holes were made by lion bites. My first reaction was a combination of revulsion and fascination.

This revulsion/fascination reaction was very common in visitors to my photo studio when they saw a specimen. Some people would cringe at the bones, especially the skulls, but then they'd want to get a closer look or touch them. There seemed to be a consensus that the teeth of carnivores held the most interest and evoked the most fear.

I've been contemplating whether or not the *Bones* experience will leave any lasting marks on me. Aside from the anatomical knowledge I gained, it has left some changes in my perceptions. Now sometimes when I look at people's faces, I can "see" through their skin to their skull and experience a feeling of voyeurism, having peeked beneath their flesh.

The other thing I carry with me from this series of photographs, and which finally became my answer to the question "why bones?" is the heightened awareness of how quickly life passes. All of these specimens were alive, interacting with their environment. Photographing them has made me think of my legacy to this planet. Will I accomplish anything lasting? Or will I merely leave a pile of bones?

Brian Kosoff
New York City

Index

Acanthicus **125**

Aceros **164**

acoustics **145**

Agout **207**

Alligator **89**, **127**, **205**

Amerindian artefacts **13, 17**

amphibians, early **195**

angel **189**

angler fish **118**

ankle **75**

antlers **14, 18, 20, 39, 163**

Apatosaurus **52, 53**

Apteryx **86**

Ara **109**

Archaeopteryx **106**

armadillo **61, 62**

aye-aye **183, 185**

baboon **116, 130, 135**

baby **166, 177**

backbones **60, 61, 63, 78**

Balaenoptera **22**

ball and socket **71, 75, 81**

bat **156, 191**

Batrachosuchus **196**

beak **108, 131, 211, 217**

beaver **143**

bichir **201**

bite force **87**

Boa **149**

bobcat **178**

bone **33, 36**

bone, cancellous (spongy) **45, 79**

Bradypus **48**

brain **177, 181**

brittleness **37**

brontosaur **52, 53**

buffalo **40, 140**

bulla, tympanic **35, 158**

caiman **88**

calcium phosphate **33**

camel **103**

camouflage **203**

cannon bone **17, 67, 186**

Capra **173**

capybara **70, 143**

Carcharodon **123**

caribou **18**

carnassial tooth **135**

carp **129, 152, 199**

cartilage **23, 77, 128**

cat **64, 65, 103, 135, 177**

"cat", native **132**

catfish **125, 128, 153, 154**

cattle **137**

Cebus **74, 182**

Cephalopus **168**

ceramics **31**

chameleon **12, 15**

chewing **71, 129, 133, 135, 143**

Chrysemys **88**

Clarias **153, 154**

claws **100, 103**

cod **60, 144**

collagen **31**

composite materials **31, 33**

cow **137**

cracks **32**

crane **159, 160**

crocodiles **129, 174, 179**

Crocodylus **174**

Crocuta **134**

Crompton. A.W. **94**

Crotalus **111**

Currey, John **36, 138**

cusps **131**

Damas **38**

dassie **90**

Dasypus **61, 62**

Dasyurus **132**

Daubentonia **183, 185**

deer **38, 76, 103, 181**

Delphinus **83**

dentine **23, 115, 137**

design **14**

Didelphis **133**

Dipodomys **158**

dinosaur **21, 161, 162, 177**

Dolichotis **30**

dolphin **16, 83, 136, 157**

dog **189**

drum fish **126, 129**

duiker **168**

eagle **59, 84, 87, 210, 212, 213, 214, 215, 216, 218**

eardrum **146, 151, 217**

ear ossicles **150, 217**

echolocation **157**

elastin **101**

Eldredge, Niles **14**

elbow **171**

elephant **138**

enamel **115, 137**

Eohippus **55**

epiphysis **90, 168, 169, 171**

Equus **66, 96, 186**

Erethizon **141**

Esox **105**

Eusthenopteron **197**

eye sockets **72, 177**

eyeball **217**

fangs **111, 130**

Felis **64**

femur **15, 43**

fiberglass **31, 32**

fibers **29**

fibula **14**

fins **80, 200**

flounder **80, 200**

flute **15**

foot, birds **24, 28**

  human **73**

  mammals **66, 74, 100, 186, 187**

  fore arm **107**

four-bar mechanism **107**

fractal **209**

fractures **52, 55**

freedom, degrees of **67, 75, 107**

frog **148**

fruit flies 200
funny bone 85, 171

Gadus 60, **144**
Galileo 181
game, pin and ring 13
gar pike 114
Gaunt, Abbott 161
gibbon 44, 56
Giraffa (giraffe) 103, **206**
gnawing 143
goat **173**
grazing 137
Griffith, A.A. 32
Grimes Graves 19
growth 167
Grus **160**

hadrosaur 162
Haliaeetus 84, 87, 210, 212, 213, 214,
    215, 216, 218
hand 69, 182, 184
Harkness, Lindsey 15
hearing 146
heel **168**
helical spirals 175
hero shrew 52
hip joint 71
holostean fishes 128
horn 23, 40, 173
hornbill 164
horse 66, 96, 137, **186**
human, baby 166
    backbone **78**
    brain 181
    ear ossicles **150**
    femur 15
    foot 73
    hand 69
    skeleton **176**
    skull 42, **208**
    tooth 137
hyaena 134
Hydrochaeris **70**

Hydrolycus 117

Ichthyostega 196
Idiurus **190**
Iguana 76, 179
impact 37
incisor **141**, 171
ivory 23, 115, 138

jaw 16, 92, 118, 123, 130, 174
jaw joints 68, **70**
jaw mechanisms 103, 108, 213
jaw muscles 94, 213
Jenkins, Farish 59
John Dory (fish) **112**
joints 59
joints, number of 75

kangaroo **187**
kangaroo rat **158**
kiwi 86, 108
knee 90, 91, **170**
knife, skinning 17

Lambeosaurus 162
Lepisosteus 114
levers 87
ligaments 31, 65, 101, 104
lion 63, 68, **100**, 103, 163, 178
lizard 76, 179
Lobodon 143
Lophius 118
loricariid catfish 128
lubrication of joints 77
lungfish 198
Lynx 178

macaw 109
Macropus **187**
Mammut 51
manatee 45, **47**

mara **30**
marrow 44
mastodon 51
mechanical advantage 88
mechanisms 101
Meleagris **170**
mirrors 203
moa 26, **28**, 52, 56
modules 200
molar 131, **137**
mole 82, 85
monkey 74, 159, **182**
Monodon 138
moose 17, 181
muscles 81
Myliobatis 124
Myleus 122
Myocastor **172**

narwhal 139
nasal passages 127
Nautilus 35, 175
neck 101, 102
necklace 13
nostrils **54**, 183
nutria 172

opossum 133
orangutan 71, 183, **184**
Ornithorhynchus 77
ostariophysan fishes 152, 199
osteoarthritis 78
Osteolaemus 179
ostrich 24, **25**, 56
otolith **144**, 152
otter, sea 54
owl 153, **155**

Pachyornis 26, 28
paca **207**
pacu 122
Panthera 63, 68, 95, 100, 178
Papio 116, 130

Paralichthys **80, 200**
Parasaurolophus **163**
parrot **108**
pattern **189, 193**
peacock **163**
pelvis **48,** 99
perch **104,** 119
petrel **171**
Phacochoerus **98**
pharyngeal teeth **126,** 129
Phocaena **180**
picks **19**
pig, bush **209**
pike **104, 105**
pineal eye **195**
piranha **120**
plant food **135**
plastics **29**
platypus **77**
Pogonias **126**
polymers **29**
Polypterus **201**
Pongo **71, 183, 184**
porcupine **141**
porpoise **180**
Potamochoerus **209**
premolar **131**
Procavia **90**
Psammobates **204**
Pseudorca **188**
Psittacosaurus **179**
Pteropus **191**
pterosaur **42**
pulleys **87,** 92
Python **10, 108, 110**

Rana **148**
Rangifer **18**
rattlesnake **111,** 131
ray **124,** 128
resonance **159**
Rhinolophus **156**
ribs **47, 55**
rodent **71,** 143, 171
rudiments **186**

safety factor **56**
sandwich construction **45, 49, 52,** 211
scales **167, 201, 203**
Scaumenacia **198**
Schmidt-Nielsen, Knut **159**
scrimshaw **16**
seal **142**
segments **200**
Serrasalmus **121**
sesamoid **171**
shark **123**
shell, mollusk **33, 34,** 175
shell, turtle **50, 204**
shoulder blade **83, 85**
Sinclair, Alice **87**
slipped disc **63**
sloth **48,** 99
snake **10, 108, 110, 111,** 131, **148,** 151
sound **145**
spear thrower **19, 20**
squirrel, flying **190**
stapes **148, 149, 150**
sternum **84, 160**
strain **32**
strength, tensile and compressive **32**
stress **31**
Struthio **24**
suction feeding **107,** 113, 119
sutures **207**
swan **159**
swift **171**
swimbladder **152**
synapsid reptiles **92, 93**
Syncerus **40, 140**
synovial fluid **77**

Talpa **82**
Tapirus (tapir) **102**
Tarsius (tarsier) **73**
tarsometatarsus **26**
teeth **115, 174,** 177
teleost fishes **128,** 167
tendons **31,** 171
texture **204**

Thrinaxodon **93**
tibia **14**
tiger **95,** 103
toad, clawed **67**
toothplates **124**
tortoise **128**
toughness **37**
Tragulus **76**
Trematops **192**
Trematosaurus **194, 196**
Trichechus **47**
Trionyx **147**
trout **119**
tubular structure **41, 46**
turkey **170**
Tursiops **136**
turtle **50, 88,** 131, **147**
tusk **139**
Tyrannosaurus **21**
Tyto **155**

universal joint **68**

vertebrae, brontosaur **53**
fish **60**
human **78**
mammals **61, 63, 102**
voice **159**

warthog **98**
Weberian ossicles **152,** 199
Weishampel, Daivd **163**
Wesley, John **15**
whalebone **22**
whale **35,** 181, **188, 189**
windpipe **161**
wing **85, 108,** 189
wishbone **59, 87**

Zeus **112**
zygapophyses **65**

Acknowledgments

I would like to thank the following people, without whom *Bones* could not have been completed.

Mark A. Norell, Department of Vertebrate Paleontology, the American Museum of Natural History, through whose good offices we obtained most of the specimens photographed for *Bones,* and the cooperation of many other people at the Museum. Mark has remained steadfastly enthusiastic about this project from beginning to end.

Others at the Museum whose support and assistance were crucial were Michael Ellison, Joan Davis, Ed Heck, Jim Clark and John Alexander of the Department of Vertebrate Paleontology; Bryn Mader, Nancy B. Simmons and Ross McPhee of the Department of Mammalogy; Allison Andors of the Department of Ornithology; Melanie L. J. Stiassny, Darrel Frost, Linda Ford and Barbara Brown of the Department of Herpetology and Ichthyology; Ian Tattersall, Jaymie L. Brauer and Stanley A. Freed of the Department of Anthropology; and Niles Eldredge of the Department of Invertebrates.

Henry Galiano, proprietor of Maxilla & Mandible Ltd., and his associates Ralph Cortes and Deborah Wan Liew. Henry early on was encouraging about *Bones* and supplied several of the specimens seen in the photographs.

Barbara Harkins, Harwood Publishing and Design, and Victor Cavalli, PIP Printing.

Natalie P. Chapman, Macmillan Publishing Company, and Anthony Cheetham, Michael Dover and Lucas Dietrich, Weidenfeld and Nicolson Publishers, for their enthusiastic support of the book.

Mrs. Janice Ruecroft, my secretary; and Mrs. Irene Poole, who has been typing my book manuscripts for more than twenty years.

Finally, I would like to thank Peter N. Nevraumont, who suggested the book and worked very hard for its success; Brian Kosoff, who took the wonderful photographs; José Conde, who graced this book with its elegant design; the late Murray Alcosser, who inspired this project; and my wife, Ann, who tolerates my devoting so much time to science.

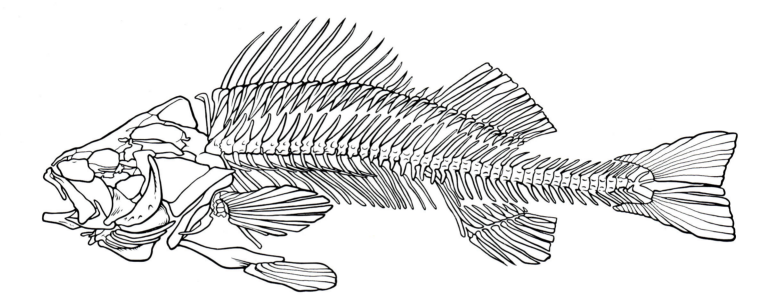

Perch skeleton
Perca flavescens
There are many more bones in the skeletons of bony
(teleost) fish than in those of mammals.